The Industrial Revolution
1760–1830

T. S. Ashton was Professor of Economic History in the University of London from 1944 to 1954, and Emeritus Professor until his death in 1968.

Pat Hudson is Professor of Economic and Social History at the University of Liverpool.

OPUS General Editors

Christopher Butler
Robert Evans
John Skorupski

OPUS books provide concise, original, and authoritative introductions to a wide range of subjects in the humanities and sciences. They are written by experts for the general reader as well as for students.

T. S. ASHTON

The Industrial Revolution
1760–1830

With a new Preface and Bibliography by Pat Hudson

Oxford New York

OXFORD UNIVERSITY PRESS

OXFORD
UNIVERSITY PRESS

Great Clarendon Street, Oxford OX2 6DP

Oxford University Press is a department of the University of Oxford.
It furthers the University's objective of excellence in research, scholarship,
and education by publishing worldwide in

Oxford New York

Athens Auckland Bangkok Bogotá Buenos Aires Calcutta
Cape Town Chennai Dar es Salaam Delhi Florence Hong Kong Istanbul
Karachi Kuala Lumpur Madrid Melbourne Mexico City Mumbai
Nairobi Paris São Paulo Singapore Taipei Tokyo Toronto Warsaw

with associated companies in Berlin Ibadan

Oxford is a registered trade mark of Oxford University Press
in the UK and in certain other countries

British Library Cataloguing in Publication Data

Data available

Library of Congress Cataloging in Publication Data

Data available

ISBN 0-19-289289-4

5 7 9 10 8 6 4

Printed in Great Britain by
Cox and Wyman Ltd
Reading, Berkshire

Preface (1997 edition)

Half-a-century has passed since Ashton wrote his short yet finely
detailed work on the industrial revolution in England.
Subsequent decades have inevitably seen major change in the
ways in which economic history is researched and written. The
discovery of new source materials, more-intensive use of evidence, shifts in the interests of historians, and the employment of
computers have stimulated much rewriting of the history of the
industrial revolution. Progress has been made in our estimation
of growth rates of national income, capital formation, industrial
output and productivity. We know a great deal more about
demographic change and the impact of industrialization upon
society and culture: living standards, political ideas and beliefs,
religion, family and personal life. We are also more likely today
to place the history of British industrialization in a comparative
and global context. Any reader steeped in the recent literature
will certainly find parts of Ashton's analysis which are now out-
dated and even misleading; but the more surprising thing is that,
after fifty years, specialists as well as students can still be stimulated by Ashton's account. One can appreciate the ways in which
he anticipated many questions which have subsequently been
debated, and benefit from a succinct analysis of major causal factors and social and cultural elements which is unclouded by more
recent (not always productive) controversy.

Ashton was born in 1899, the third child of the manager of the
Trustee Savings Bank in Ashton-Under-Lyne.[1] He was based at

---

[1] Biographical information is drawn from the *Dictionary of National Biography, Supplement
1961–1970* (1972). The entry is written by D. C. Coleman.

the University of Manchester for much of his professional life, although for the decade before his retirement in 1954 he held the Chair in Economic History at the London School of Economics. His thrifty, Nonconformist, and middle-class upbringing in the industrial north-west was stamped upon his historical work: his pragmatic and practical approach; his accessible and unpretentious style; his major interest in Nonconformity, and industrial and financial history; his economic liberalism and his interest in those caught up in the dislocations and poverty of changing times. This background and these qualities set Ashton and his work apart from most of his contemporaries. But his work also stands out because Ashton wrote with such great lucidity and obvious enthusiasm. Perhaps because of his early background in teaching trade-unionists, he wrote for an audience wider than professional academics. He chose to publish his book in the Home University of Modern Knowledge series with Oxford University Press. Like the Dent Everyman volumes and the Pelican books of the interwar and post-war years, the objective of the series was to provide accessible material of high scholarship to the 'interested general public'. In the 1940s and 1950s, before the expansion of higher education, this interested public was sizeable and its appetite voracious. By directing his work at this readership Ashton differed from most of his contemporaries in the élite of the historical profession. The light and lucid touch of *The Industrial Revolution* also differs markedly from most of what is written on this subject today, which addresses a closed and narrow, technical readership.

Whilst Ashton's audience and style make his book accessible and much more pleasurable to read than most modern academic literature, the absence of footnotes and references to primary and secondary source materials makes the work tantalizing for the modern scholar. There are clear signs of the influence of earlier work by P. Mantoux, J. H. Clapham, G. Unwin, I. Pinchbeck, H. Heaton, E. Gilboy, A. P. Wadsworth, and J. de L. Mann, among others, and Ashton's debt to H. L. Beales, F. J. Fisher, F. Collier, A. H. John, and W. W. Rostow is acknowledged in the Preface. One can also identify sections of the work which embody the use of original sources such as

Parliamentary Reports, business records and family papers, most obviously in discussion of coal-mining, iron and steel manufacture, industrial organization generally, commercial credit, and the social and religious background of entrepreneurs. But it would be very useful and interesting, as an exercise in historiographical analysis and lineage, to be able to identify more clearly the points of overlap between Ashton and his predecessors and contemporaries. It would also be useful to be able to check the sources for some of Ashton's more contentious and unsupported pronouncements such as '[the emergence of] a single, increasingly sensitive, market for labour' by 1830 (p. 101).

In order to benefit fully from a reading of *The Industrial Revolution* in the late 1990s, it is useful to consider the extent to which aspects of Ashton's analysis have been modified or overturned by subsequent research. In a much-quoted phrase from his Introduction, Ashton is in no doubt that 'the face of England changed' and that the changes were 'not merely "industrial", but also social and intellectual' (p. 2). In this his approach differs from much recent economic history which has tended to stress continuity and gradualism and, has concentrated upon macroeconomic indicators and economic issues in isolation from political, social, and cultural events and changes. Ashton recognized that economic processes were not characterized by sudden change and that the industrial revolution was just one stage, and not the last, in a much longer process of capitalist development. Nevertheless, his account resounds with discussion of the revolutionary shifts occurring in the economy and society of late eighteenth- and early nineteenth-century England. It is this which makes the work such a fascinating read.

The nature and impact of population growth is both a central theme in Ashton's account and has received a great deal of attention from specialist researchers over subsequent decades. Ashton's acceptance that 'it was a fall in mortality that led to increase of numbers' was for several decades bolstered by studies of improvements in living standards, food distribution, and medicine, especially smallpox vaccination. However, Wrigley and Schofield's pathbreaking work, *The Population History of England, 1541–1871* (1981), overturned ideas on the subject through a detailed aggregative study of registers from over 400 parishes. Their results indicated that fertility changes were two-and-a-half times more important than changes in mortality in accounting for demographic increase in the eighteenth century. Since 1981 most demographic research has concentrated on the mainsprings of nuptiality and fertility change. Some, like Wrigley and Schofield, relate lower marriage ages and higher marriage rates primarily to changing real incomes, others to shifting employment prospects and practices, to proletarian (as opposed to 'peasant') demographic regimes, to migration, and to greater social and sexual freedoms for young people. However, it is likely that Wrigley and Schofield's assessment of the significance of improvement in background mortality rates is unduly low. We know that towns had much higher mortality rates than the countryside and that in 1670 13.5 per cent of the population lived in towns with populations over 5,000 compared with 21 per cent in 1770 and 27.5 per cent by 1801. The fact that average aggregate life-expectancy increased by about six years between c.1680 and 1820 is therefore remarkable. Shifts in fertility may appear more significant, in accounting for overall population growth, at the aggregate level. But, bearing in mind the redistribution of the population in favour of towns, with their higher mortality penalty, it is not surprising that we are currently witnessing a return to emphasis upon the mortality improvements which so concerned Ashton.

In his chapter on earlier forms of industry Ashton examines the nature of pre-factory manufacturing, which has come under scrutiny in recent years not least from historians considering the concept of proto-industrialization (an initial phase of industrialization characterized by the dynamic effects of the spread of rural domestic manufacturing). Ashton commented upon the movement of manufacturing away from the more restrictive institutional and social environment of towns in the early modern period and placed stress upon the 'bewildering' variety and flexibility of rural forms of domestic production. In doing so, he highlighted factors which were to become the focus of intense research in the 1970s and 1980s; as were the relationships between employers and workers which Ashton also considered:

the provision of tools and equipment, the nature of the wage, truck and 'long-pay', subcontracting, middlemen, indebtedness, embezzlement, family units of production, underemployment. To the modern reader it is surprising that Ashton pays relatively little attention to the relationship between industrialization and changes in agriculture which may have provoked or retarded both rural manufacture and the wider growth of incomes, consumer spending, and transport and financial infrastructures. Although debate still rages over the net contribution of agriculture to industrialization, the literature on this is much fuller now than in 1948.

Another factor in English industrialization which was stressed by Ashton is the importance of relatively cheap capital. He argues that the lowering rate of interest in the second half of the eighteenth century expedited the construction of mines, canals, factories, and houses and that this was perhaps the most important single factor promoting the quickening pace of economic development. We now know much more about the supply of capital in the eighteenth century; about the growth of, and controversies surrounding, the national debt; about the extent of crowding out of civilian investment in the Napoleonic War years; the geographically and socially fragmented nature of industrial capital markets; the importance for industrialists and traders of personal and family contacts and of long credits, at variable interest, which could help to tide manufacturers over lengthy periods of realization. National-level indicators of interest rates are now seen as less helpful indicators of the supply and cost of capital (for industry at least) than Ashton suggested.

Chapter 3 on technical innovations is in some respects old fashioned, with its catalogue of major technical breakthroughs in agricultural and industrial production and the potted histories of great men. Subsequent research has emphasized the countless, largely anonymous, modifications of innovations which made them workable or more efficient and has begun to focus upon the importance of product innovation and design as well as innovation in production methods. However, Ashton himself emphasized that discovery is not the achievement of individual genius. He argued that innovation was a social and cultural as well as an

economic process, a product of society in the round as much as
of great men or of supply-and-demand curves. In Schumpeterian
mould and in an approach later extended variously by Kuznets
and Mokyr, Ashton looks at the factors which influenced innovative activity: capital supplies, war, peace, and economic cycles,
links between industries, bottlenecks, and, perhaps most import-
antly, a framework of law and institutions protecting private
property rights. Ashton's account of the economic and social
implications of innovative activity, especially in the iron and textile industries, remains a classic which anticipates later research
by emphasizing new regional concentrations and the rise of new
types of communities as well as the technical aspects of change
in industrial processes. The links between economic factors and
social change are emphasized, and in ways which would benefit
even now from further research:

timing apart, it is important in each case to be clear whether the effect
[of innovation] was to substitute natural resources or capital for labour,
labour for capital, or one kind of labour for another. For on this
depended the distribution, not merely among factors of production, but
also among the different social classes, of the increased wealth to which
the inventions gave rise. (p. 74)

His paragraphs on the importance of canal construction and on
the timing and impact of waves of innovative activity are classic
examples of Ashton's incisive style: his ability to convey so many
ideas in just a sentence or two.

In his chapter on capital and labour Ashton explores the structure of enterprises and the culture of entrepreneurship.
Famously, he emphasizes the relationship between entrepreneurial endeavour, capital accumulation, and religious nonconformity, especially Quakerism, which provoked much subsequent
research. Considerable attention is also paid to changes in credit
practices in trade: the use of bills of exchange, the growth of
banking, the rise of the Stock Exchange and of bill broking.
Ashton's view, expressed in this context, that 'A new sense of
time was one of the outstanding psychological features of the
industrial revolution' (p. 80) has been taken up in a wide range
of subsequent studies of work-discipline, social protest, and cul-

tural values and horizons, as well as in research upon credit and capital turnover.

Ashton's treatment of labour is integrated into his general discussion of industrial expansion and change. He is writing before the (in some ways unfortunate) rise of a separate labour history on the one hand and econometric history on the other, and before the damaging bifurcation between social and economic history hardened from the 1960s. His discussion of the recruitment, organization, and control of labour in centralized production anticipates aspects of Pollard's *Genesis of Modern Management* (1965). Ashton stresses that the rise of regimented work and factory discipline were 'as much a part of the revolution as the technical inventions themselves' (p. 99); a view which has subsequently held. In describing the provision of housing and social amenity for industrial workers, altruism and charity are the motives primarily stressed by Ashton, although he also discusses economic imperatives such as the labour shortage and remote sites of early factories. There is no mention of notions of social control or hegemony which had yet to be developed in historical analysis. Neither is there any attempt to differentiate between male and female experience. This was not to occur until the growth of women's history and the employment of the concept of gender from the 1970s. Although Pinchbeck had provided a rich source of information on changes in female work as early as 1930, Ashton and his contemporaries drew upon it only a little.

Ashton has empathy with the plight of young workers, their 'neglect, promiscuity, and degradation' (p. 91), but such workers remain an anonymous mass compared with the industrial and commercial élite. There is no sign here of that attitude to sources or to the voiceless which was later to yield a new 'history from below', nor any questioning of the inequities or distributional inefficiencies inherent in the market system. Ashton thus represents an entirely separate tradition to that of either the Christian socialists like the Hammonds and Tawney (though it was Tawney who sponsored Ashton's move to LSE), or of the Historians Group of the Communist Party of Great Britain whose work was an important foundation of modern English

social history. In the mould of J. H. Clapham, Ashton represents
the tradition of empiricism and economic liberalism, in his case
tempered by an empathetic interest in social problems and by a
more fully integrated approach to the study of economic and
social life. Although Ashton recognizes and documents ill effects
and abuses which flowed from rapid industrial change and
urbanization, he was generally an optimist about both the short-
and longer-term effects of industrialization, including the impact
of change upon the living standards of the mass of the population. In this he also followed Clapham. He argued that many of
the abuses of employment of women and children, as well as
men, which were revealed in parliamentary enquiries of the
1830s and 1840s were dying out as the result of economic development. In addition, work discipline, fines, abuses were 'the price
workers had to pay for the higher incomes that large-scale industry brought' (p. 99). And where change appeared unduly painful,
exogenous factors or interference with the market mechanism
are highlighted. Ashton's market-oriented, modernizing, and
progressive framework of analysis has floated in and out of
favour in more recent decades but lines up rather well with much
current analysis. Ashton's discussion of the slow decline of hand-
weaving, for example, suggests that transfer to factory production
was slowed and made more painful because of both Poor Relief
provision and immigration. Similar factors are currently stressed
in relation to the slow pace of structural change and high unemployment in late twentieth-century Britain.

In his penultimate, very short, chapter Ashton highlights the
social, cultural, and political aspects of economic change. he
attacks the notion that the age was characterized by the rise of
self-centred and avaricious individualism. He stresses the ideals
and practices of association, community, and voluntarism as
hallmarks of the industrial revolution, but he also documents the
collusions, price-fixing, and monopolies fostered by association-
ism amongst industrialists and employers. The many forms of
expression of a corporate sense of labour are more briefly
addressed. The history of the entrepreneurial middle class and its
culture and institutions has been the subject of a deal of study
since Ashton's time, and the history of organized labour has been

the main feature of English social history until recent years. Thus, Ashton addressed the concerns which were to dominate the literature on the social history of industrialization in England for the following half-century. The chapter finally contains an uncharacteristically uncertain view of the extent and impact of '*laisser-faire*'. Ashton appears critical of the ideal of minimal government, rightly suggests that practice never matched the nineteenth-century ideals, but then states that a more interventionist state would have done little to prevent social problems, poverty, dislocation, and disorder because the supply of efficient administrators, health officials, and civil servants was not forthcoming until later. The deleterious impact of industrialization on the mass of population is attributed to 'defects of administrative, and not of economic, processes' (p. 113): a notion which still awaits full historical investigation.

Chapter 6 adopts a chronological rather than a thematic approach and attempts to consider longer-term movements of prices and outputs, of currency and capital supply. Surprisingly, but mirroring the scant treatment of domestic demand, there is little development of the role of foreign trade in industrialization nor any full analysis of the factors which lay behind the expansion of overseas commerce. In the tradition of economic history which has always dominated the literature, Ashton was very much a historian of production and supply-side changes. Today much more attention is being paid to changing consumption patterns and habits, which are seen not just to reflect supply-side shifts but also as a driving force in the industrialization process. In considering the role of foreign trade in providing cheap imports of food and raw materials and creating profits for investment elsewhere in the economy, Ashton's analysis is also very limited. The slave trade, for example, gets no mention despite the publication in 1944 of Eric Williams's classic work, *Capitalism and Slavery*. There has been much subsequent debate and research on these issues. This chapter is also striking, especially in comparison with work on the subject today, because it contains very little quantitative evidence: there are no graphs or tables of figures, even though sufficient data was available to give a firmer indication of general movements as they were then understood. Periodic crises in the output of both agriculture and industry, investment, and employment are highlighted, as is the impact of various periods of war. The economic, social, and political effects of the Napoleonic Wars are a focus of attention. In counterfactual vein, Ashton suggests that:

if statesmen had directed their attention to providing a stable standard of value and a proper medium of exchange; if there had been no wars to force up prices, raise rates of interest, and turn resources to destruction, the course of the industrial revolution would have been smoother, and its consequences would not have been, as they are, in dispute. (p. 126)

The chapter then returns to the impact of industrialization on the standard of living of the mass of population, which helped to spark the most vitriolic and ideologically loaded debate amongst economic historians this century. Ashton's cautiously optimistic contribution again fails to present much quantitative evidence but is a model of close and logical reasoning coupled with literary imagery and an indelible belief in the progress of the age.

Ashton retired thirteen years before I arrived at the London School of Economics as an undergraduate in 1967, and he died the following year. His influence at the School remained strong in subsequent decades, where it blended with the entirely different legacy of Tawney to produce a curious but stimulating hybrid. Ashton's emphasis on the need to refer to first principles of economic analysis in attempting to understand economic and social relationships in the past was particularly strongly emulated. Although I was too late to experience Ashton's renowned seminars, where 'penetrating and pertinent questions were gently delivered in a Lancashire accent and through a fog of cigarette smoke',[2] reading his books and becoming familiar with his style was a formative influence on all economic historians of my generation.

Pat Hudson

Liverpool
1996

---

[2] Biographical information is drawn from the *Dictionary of National Biography, Supplement 1961–1970* (1972). The entry is written by D. C. Coleman, 37.

Contents

1

Introduction

IN THE short span of years between the accession of George III and that of his son, William IV, the face of England changed. Areas that for centuries had been cultivated as open fields, or had lain untended as common pasture, were hedged or fenced; hamlets grew into populous towns; and chimney stacks rose to dwarf the ancient spires. Highroads were made—straighter, stronger, and wider than those evil communications that had corrupted the good manners of travellers in the days of Defoe. The North and Irish Seas, and the navigable reaches of the Mersey, Ouse, Trent, Severn, Thames, Forth, and Clyde were joined together by threads of still water. In the North the first iron rails were laid down for the new locomotives, and steam packets began to ply on the estuaries and the narrow seas.

Parallel changes took place in the structure of society. The number of people increased vastly, and the proportion of children and young probably rose. The growth of new communities shifted the balance of population from the South and East to the North and Midlands; enterprising Scots headed a procession the end of which is not yet in sight; and a flood of unskilled, but vigorous, Irish poured in, not without effect on the health and ways of life of Englishmen. Men and women born and bred in the countryside came to live crowded together, earning their bread, no longer as families or groups of neighbours, but as units in the labour force of factories; work grew to be more specialized; new forms of skill were developed, and some old forms lost. Labour became more mobile, and higher standards of comfort were offered to those able and willing to move to centres of opportunity.

At the same time fresh sources of raw material were exploited, new markets were opened, and new methods of trade devised. Capital increased in volume and fluidity; the currency was set on a gold base; a banking system came into being. Many old privileges and monopolies were swept away, and legislative impediments to enterprise removed. The State came to play a less active, the individual and the voluntary association a more active, part in affairs. Ideas of innovation and progress undermined traditional sanctions: men began to look forward, rather than backward, and their thoughts as to the nature and purpose of social life were transformed.

Whether or not such a series of changes should be spoken of as 'The Industrial Revolution' might be debated at length. The changes were not merely 'industrial', but also social and intellectual. The word 'revolution' implies a suddenness of change that is not, in fact, characteristic of economic processes. The system of human relationships that is sometimes called capitalism had its origins long before 1760, and attained its full development long after 1830: there is a danger of overlooking the essential fact of continuity. But the phrase 'Industrial Revolution' has been used by a long line of historians and has become so firmly embedded in common speech that it would be pedantic to offer a substitute.

The outstanding feature of the social history of the period— the thing that above all others distinguishes the age from its predecessors—is the rapid growth of population. Careful estimates, based on figures of burials and christenings, put the number of people in England and Wales at about five and a half millions in 1700, and six and a half millions in 1750: when the first census was taken in 1801 it was a round nine millions, and by 1831 had reached fourteen millions. In the second half of the eighteenth century population had thus increased by 40 per cent, and in the first three decades of the nineteenth century by more than 50 per cent. For Great Britain the figures are approximately eleven millions in 1801, and sixteen and a half millions in 1831.

The growth of population was not the result of any marked change in the birth-rate. During the first four decades of the eighteenth century, it is true, the number of births per thousand people seems to have risen a little. Farm labourers tended to set up households of their own instead of boarding with their employers, and a decline of the system of apprenticeship in industry also led to earlier marriage and larger families. But from 1740 to 1830 the birth-rate appears to have fluctuated only very slightly: for no decade does the estimate rise above 37·7, or fall below 36·6. Throughout the industrial revolution fertility was high but steady.

Nor can the increase of people be attributed to an influx from other countries. In every decade men and women took ship from Ireland to England and Scotland, and at times of dearth the trickle became a stream. But there was no such torrent of Irish immigration as was to come in the last five years of the 1840s. On the other hand, during the eighteenth century perhaps a million people left Britain to seek a living overseas, mainly in the colonies. Among them were some 50,000 criminals transported to Maryland or Botany Bay, and a number of artisans who defied the law by carrying their technical knowledge and skill to Europe—not in the long run, it may be guessed, to the disadvantage of their native land. On balance, Britain was not a receiving centre but a breeding-ground for new communities across the seas.

It was a fall in mortality that led to the increase of numbers. In the first four decades of the eighteenth century excessive indulgence in cheap gin and intermittent periods of famine and disease took a heavy toll of lives; but between 1740 and 1820 the death-rate fell almost continuously—from an estimated 35·8 for the ten years ending in 1740 to one of 21·1 for those ending in 1821. Many influences were operating to reduce the incidence of death. The introduction of root crops made it possible to feed more cattle in the winter months, and so to supply fresh meat throughout the year. The substitution of wheat for inferior cereals, and an increased consumption of vegetables, strengthened resistance to disease. Higher standards of personal cleanliness, associated with more soap and cheaper cotton underwear, lessened the dangers of infection. The use of brick in place of timber in the walls, and of slate or stone instead of thatch in the roofs of cottages, reduced the number of pests; and the removal of many noxious processes of manufacture from the homes of the workers brought greater domestic comfort. The larger towns were paved, drained, and supplied with running water; knowledge of medicine and surgery developed; hospitals and dispensaries increased; and more attention was paid to such things as the disposal of refuse and the proper burial of the dead.

Since there are no reliable statistics it is not possible to say which age groups of the population benefited most from these improvements. In a well-known passage of his autobiography Edward Gibbon says:

> The death of a new-born child before that of its parents may seem an unnatural, but it is strictly a probable event; since of any given number, the greater part are extinguished before their ninth year, before they possess the faculties of mind or body. Without accusing the profuse waste or imperfect workmanship of Nature, I shall only observe that this unfavourable chance was multiplied against my infant existence. So feeble was my constitution, so precarious my life, that in the baptism of each of my brothers, my father's prudence repeated my Christian name of Edward, that in case of the departure of the eldest son, this patronymic appellation might be still perpetuated in the family.

This was written in 1792–3. By that time it is probable that the profuse waste of infant life was a little less than at the date of Gibbon's birth, and, if so, there would be a higher percentage of children and young people in the population. It is a matter to be borne in mind in considering the constitution of the labour force of the early factories.

The increase of the population of Britain occurred at a time when the output of commodities was also increasing at a rapid rate, and this coincidence has led to hasty generalizations. Some writers have drawn the inference that it was the growth of industry that led to the growth of numbers. If this were true the growth of industry must have exerted its influence, not through the birth-rate (which, as we have seen, remained steady), but through the death-rate. Some of the improvements in the arts of living mentioned above certainly depended on a development of industry, but it would be rash to assign to this a major part in the reduction of mortality. For population was growing rapidly, not only in Britain, but also in most other countries of western and northern Europe, where nothing in the nature of an industrial revolution occurred.

Other writers, reversing the causal sequence, have declared that the growth of population, through its effect on the demand for commodities, stimulated the expansion of industry. An increase of people, however, does not necessarily mean either a greater effective demand for manufactured goods or an increased production of these in the country concerned. (If it did we should expect to find a rapid economic development of Ireland in the eighteenth, and of Egypt, India, and China in the nineteenth century.) It may just as well lead to a lower standard of life for all. The spectre of the pressure of population on the means of subsistence which oppressed the mind of Malthus in 1798 was no chimera. It is true that the immediate pressure was less than Malthus supposed. But if, after the middle of the nineteenth century, there had been no railways in America, no opening up of the prairies, and no steamships, Britain might have learnt from bitter experience the fallacy of the view that, because with every pair of hands there is a mouth, therefore every expansion of numbers must lead to an increase of consumption and so of output. In Britain, in the eighteenth century and later, it so happened that, alongside the increase of population, there was taking place an increase of the other factors of production, and hence it was possible for the standard of life of the people—or of most of them—to rise.

There was an increase in the acreage of land under cultivation. Much attention was given to the draining of fens and marshes, to the breaking up and turning to arable of the old, rough, common pastures (which were usually spoken of as the waste), and to the hedging of land, so as to make it more productive of both crops and livestock. 'In this manner', wrote an observer of these developments, 'was more useful territory added to the empire, at the expence of individuals, than had been gained by every war since the Revolution.' Several new crops were introduced. The turnip made it possible to increase the size of the herds of cattle, and the potato, which was becoming a popular food in the North, brought substantial economies in the use of land. More will be said later about the agricultural and agrarian changes. It is sufficient here to make the point that land previously outside the system of economic activities was being drawn in, and put to better use. The lines of the moving frontier can be discerned on the hillsides today by those with eyes to see.

At the same time there was taking place a rapid increase of capital. The number of people with incomes more than sufficient to cover the primary needs of life was growing: the power to save was increasing. Stable political and social conditions, following the settlement of 1688, encouraged men to look to more distant horizons: what economists call time-preference was favourable to accumulation. The class structure also was favourable to it. It is generally recognized that more saving takes place in communities in which the distribution of wealth is uneven than in those in which it approaches more closely to modern conceptions of what is just. Estimates of statisticians, from Gregory King in 1688 to Colquhoun in 1812, exhibit wide variations in the incomes of different social classes; and the rise of new institutions, including that of the National Debt, intensified the disparities that had been handed down from earlier generations.

The public debt, as we know it today, arose out of the exigencies of the wars of William III. It grew steadily—almost entirely as the result of successive wars—until, by 1815, it had reached a figure of £861 millions. Not all of it was held by the British people themselves: in 1776, perhaps a quarter or more of it was in the hands of the Dutch. But, after 1781, when Holland became involved in war with Britain, the great bulk of the debt came to be held in this country—by noblemen, squires, lawyers, retired merchants, and widows and spinsters of the well-to-do classes. In 1815 perhaps about one-eleventh, and in 1827 (according to the estimate of Sir Henry Parnell) one-twelfth, of the money income of the people of the United Kingdom consisted of sums raised from the taxpayers, including the poor, and transferred to the relatively rich holders of government bonds. In this way, increasingly, wealth came into the hands of those whose propensity was to save, rather than to spend.

Accumulation does not of itself, however, lead to the creation of capital goods: it was not only a willingness to save, but also a willingness to employ savings productively, that increased at this time. In the early eighteenth century, landlords had used saved resources to improve their own estates, merchants to extend their markets, and manufacturers to engage more labour; and some of the savings of the retired and leisured classes had been lent on mortgage to local landowners, farmers or tradesmen, or invested in the shares of a turnpike trust. Gradually the market for capital widened, aided by the rise of country bankers (who existed long before they took the name). The offer by the State of a mass of gilt-edged stock accustomed men to the idea of impersonal investment, and so they came to put their savings into enterprises distant in space and speculative in character. That the results might not always be advantageous was made manifest when the South Sea Bubble burst in 1720 and brought ruin to thousands. But, in general, the increased mobility of capital was socially beneficial, leading as it did to a substantial fall in the rate of interest.

For centuries the attitude of the State to the taking of interest had been one of hostility or, at least, of suspicion. The State was an habitual debtor—and laws had been passed prohibiting the making of loans at more than a prescribed rate. In 1625 the legal rate had been lowered from 10 to 8 per cent; in 1651 it was reduced to 6, and in 1714 to 5—in each case following upon a fall in the 'natural' rate. In the early eighteenth century the abundance of loanable funds made it possible for finance ministers to reduce the interest paid to the creditors of the State. During the wars, the Government of William III had been obliged to offer 7 or 8 per cent (the Usury Laws did not apply to the State); but in 1717 the rate on the perpetual annuities was reduced to 5, and in 1727 to 4 per cent. Finally, in the 1750s, Pelham lowered it once more, and, by converting a number of issues into a single one, brought into being, in 1757, the 3 per cent Consolidated Stock which, for short, we call Consols. These conversions were not imposed on an unwilling public; they reflected, rather than initiated, a fall of the rate of interest in the community generally. There was, at this period, no single market rate to which reference can be made, but the process can be observed in the rising price of Bank of England stock; and the ledgers of merchants and manufacturers afford further evidence of what was taking place. Much economic activity at this time was controlled by small groups of partners, each of whom was entitled either to receive his share of the annual profits or to leave it, wholly or in part, to earn interest in the concern. During the early part of the eighteenth century the rate allowed on money reinvested in this way was falling steadily. A firm of ironmasters of Worcestershire, Edward Knight and Company, for example, credited each partner with 5 per cent on the undistributed profit during the twenties and early thirties, but in 1735 the rate was reduced to 4, and in 1756 to as little as 3 per cent. If a group of men were considering the investment of their savings in some new, large capital enterprise, such as a turnpike, they would first make an estimate of the number of years it would take for their capital to be restored to them in full. If the current rate of interest were 5 per cent it would be worth while embarking on an undertaking that would return the capital in twenty years; at 4 per cent investment might be extended to one that would take twenty-five years, and at 3 per cent to one that would take up to thirty-three and a third years, to reimburse the initial outlay. The lower the rate at which capital could be obtained—the smaller the advantage forgone in locking it up in a fixed form—the further would capital works be extended.

As early as 1668 Sir Josiah Child remarked that 'all countries are at this day richer or poorer in an exact proportion to what they pay, and have usually paid, for the Interest of Money'. He went on to observe that 'the bringing down of Interest from 6 to 4, or 3 per cent will necessarily . . . double the Capital Stock of the Nation' and added that 'the Nobility and Gentry, whose estates lie mostly in Land, may presently upon all they have,

instead of fifty write one hundred'. In spite of this early exposi-
tion of the relation between interest, capital, and well-being,
the importance of the lowering of the rate of interest in the
half-century before the industrial revolution has never been
properly stressed by historians. If we seek—it would be wrong
to do so—for a single reason why the pace of economic development quickened about the middle of the eighteenth century, it is to this we must look. The deep mines, solidly built
factories, well-constructed canals, and substantial houses of
the industrial revolution were the products of relatively cheap
capital.

One thing more was necessary: the increasing supplies of
labour, land, and capital had to be co-ordinated. The eighteenth and early nineteenth centuries were rich in entrepreneurs, quick to devise new combinations of productive factors,
eager to find new markets, receptive to new ideas. 'The age is
running mad after innovation', said Dr. Johnson; 'all the business of the world is to be done in a new way; men are to be
hanged in a new way; Tyburn itself is not safe from the fury of
innovation.' The sentiments and attitudes of mind of the period
were propitious. The religious and political differences that
had torn society apart in the two preceding centuries had been
composed; and if the eighteenth century was not markedly an
age of faith, at least it practised the Christian virtue of toler-
ance. The regulation of industry by gilds, municipalities, and
the central government had broken down or had been allowed
to sleep, and the field was open for the exercise of initiative and
enterprise. It was perhaps no accident that it was in Lancashire
and the West Riding, which had been exempted from some of
the more restrictive provisions of the Elizabethan code of industrial legislation, that the development was most marked. It
was certainly no accident that it was the villages and unincor-
porated towns—places like Manchester and Birmingham—
that grew most rapidly, for industry and trade had long been
moving away from the areas where some remnants of public
control were still in operation.

During the seventeenth century the attitude of the Law had
changed: from the time of Coke judgements in the courts of

Common Law had become tender indeed to the rights of property, but hostile to privilege. In 1624 the Statute of Monopolies had swept away many vested interests, and a century and a half later Adam Smith was able to say of Englishmen that they were 'to their great honour of all peoples, the least subject to the wretched spirit of monopoly'. Whether or not the patent system, the lines of which had been laid down by that same Statute, was stimulating to innovation in industrial practice is not easy to determine. It gave security to the inventor, but it allowed some privileged positions to be maintained for an undue length of time, and it was sometimes used to block the way to new contrivance: for nearly a quarter of a century, for example, James Watt was able to prevent other engineers from constructing new types of steam engine, even under licence from himself. Many manufacturers—not all from disinterested motives—opposed the application of the law and encouraged piracy. Associations were brought into being in Manchester and other centres of industry to contest the legality of rights claimed by patentees. The Society for the Encouragement of Arts, Manufactures and Commerce, founded in 1754, offered premiums to inventors who were willing to put their devices at the free disposal of all. And Parliament itself made awards (for example, £14,000 to Thomas Lombe when his patent for silk-throwing expired, £30,000 to Jenner for the discovery of vaccine inoculation, £10,000 to Edmund Cartwright for various contrivances, and £5,000 to Samuel Crompton for his invention of the 'mule') in addition to the substantial annual grants it voted for the use of the Board of Agriculture and the Veterinary College. Without any such monetary incentive, one of the outstanding industrialists, Josiah Wedgwood, resolved 'to be released from these degrading slavish chains, these mean, selfish fears of other people copying my works'; and, at a later stage, the inventors of the safety lamps, Sir Humphry Davy, Dr. Clanny, and George Stephenson, all refused, in the interest of the miners, to take out patents for their devices. It is at least possible that without the apparatus of the patent system discovery might have developed quite as rapidly as it did.

Some accounts of the technological revolution begin with the story of a dreamy boy watching the steam raise the lid of the kettle on the domestic hearth, or with that of a poor weaver gazing with stupefaction at his wife's spinning wheel, over-turned on the floor but still revolving. These, needless to say, are nothing but romantic fiction. Other accounts leave the im-pression that the inventions were the work of obscure mill-wrights, carpenters, or clockmakers, untutored in principles, who stumbled by chance on some device that was destined to bring others to fame and fortune and themselves to penury. It is true that there were inventors—men like Brindley and Murdoch—who were endowed with little learning, but with much native wit. It is true that there were others, such as Crompton and Cort, whose discoveries transformed whole in-dustries, but left them to end their days in relative poverty. It is true that a few new products came into being as the result of accident. But such accounts have done harm by obscuring the fact that systematic thought lay behind most of the innovations in industrial practice, by making it appear that the distribution of awards and penalties in the economic system was wholly irrational, and, above all, by overstressing the part played by chance in technical progress. 'Chance', as Pasteur said, 'favours only the mind which is prepared': most discoveries are achieved only after repeated trial and error. Many involve two or more previously independent ideas or processes, which, brought together in the mind of the inventor, issue in a more or less complex and efficient mechanism. In this way, for ex-ample, the principle of the jenny was united by Crompton with that of spinning by rollers to produce the mule; and the iron rail, which had long been in use in the coal mine, was joined to the locomotive to create the railway. In such cases of what has been called cross-mutation the part played by chance must have been very small indeed.

Yet other accounts of the industrial revolution are mislead-ing because they present discovery as the achievement of in-dividual genius, and not as a social process. 'Invention', as a distinguished modern scientist, Michael Polanyi, has re-marked, 'is a drama enacted on a crowded stage.' The applause tends to be given to those who happen to be on the boards in the final act, but the success of the performance depends on the close co-operation of many players, and of those behind the scenes. The men who, together, whether as rivals or as associates, created the technique of the industrial revolution were plain Englishmen or Scots,

> Being neither demigods nor heroes,
> But ingenious, hard-working descendants of *homo sapiens*,
> Who had the luck to plant their seedlings in fine weather,
> Not in the frost or storm, but when the slow ripening of time, the
>   felicitous crossing of circumstance
> Presented unimagined opportunities,
> Which they seized. . . .

(The words are those of a master cotton-spinner, Godfrey Armitage, of our own day.)

Invention appears at every stage of human history, but it rarely thrives in a community of simple peasants or unskilled manual labourers: only when division of labour has developed, so that men devote themselves to a single product or process, does it come to harvest. Such division of labour already existed when the eighteenth century opened, and the industrial revolution was in part cause, and in part effect, of a heightening and extension of the principle of specialization.

Invention, again, is more likely to arise in a community that sets store by things of the mind than in one that seeks only material ends. The stream of English scientific thought, issuing from the teaching of Francis Bacon, and enlarged by the genius of Boyle and Newton, was one of the main tributaries of the industrial revolution. Newton, indeed, was too good a philosopher and scholar to care whether or not the ideas he gave to the world were immediately 'useful'; but the belief in the possibility of achieving industrial progress by the method of observation and experiment came to the eighteenth century largely through him. Natural philosophy was shaking itself free from its association with metaphysics and—again the application of the principle of division of labour—splitting up into the separate systems of physiology, chemistry, physics, geology and so on. The sciences were not yet, however, so specialized as to be out of contact with the language, thought, and practice of ordinary men. It was as a result of a visit to Norfolk, where he had gone to study the new methods of farming, that the Scottish landowner, James Hutton, became interested in the constitution of soils; and the discoveries that made him the most famous geologist of his day owed something to the navvies who were cutting the clays and blasting the rock to provide England with canals. Physicists and chemists, such as Franklin, Black, Priestley, Dalton, and Davy, were in intimate contact with the leading figures in British industry: there was much coming and going between the laboratory and the workshop, and men like James Watt, Josiah Wedgwood, William Reynolds, and James Keir were at home in the one as in the other. The names of engineers, ironmasters, industrial chemists, and instrument-makers on the list of Fellows of the Royal Society show how close were the relations between science and practice at this time.

Inventors, contrivers, industrialists, and entrepreneurs—it is not easy to distinguish one from another at a period of rapid change—came from every social class and from all parts of the country. Aristocrats, like Lord Lovell, in the early part of the century, and Coke of Holkham in the later, initiated improvements in agriculture; others, such as the Duke of Bridgewater and Earl Gower, created new forms of transport; and yet others were responsible for innovations in the chemical and mining industries. Clergymen and parsons, including Edmund Cartwright and Joseph Dawson, forsook the cure of souls to find out more efficient ways of weaving cloth and smelting iron. Doctors of medicine, among whom were John Roebuck and James Keir, took to chemical research and became captains of large-scale industry. Under the influence of a rationalist philosophy, scholars turned from the humanities to physical science, and some from physical science to technology. Lawyers, soldiers, public servants, and men of humbler station than these found in manufacture possibilities of advancement far greater than those offered in their original callings. A barber, Richard Arkwright, became the wealthiest and most influential of the cotton-spinners; an innkeeper, Peter Stubs, built up a highly esteemed concern in the file trade; a schoolmaster, Samuel Walker, became the leading figure in the north of England iron industry. 'Every man', exclaimed the ebullient William Hutton in 1780, 'has his fortune in his own hands.' That, it is needless to say, has never been true, or even half true; but anyone who looks closely at English society in the mid- and late eighteenth century will understand how it was possible for it to be said, for at this time vertical mobility had reached a degree higher than that of any earlier, or perhaps any succeeding, age.

It has often been observed that the growth of industry was connected historically with the rise of groups which dissented from the Church by law established in England. In the seventeenth century the congregation of Puritans gathered about Richard Baxter at Kidderminster included the Foleys, the Crowleys, and the Hanburys, who were to set up great establishments in places as far afield as Staffordshire, Durham, and South Wales. In the following century members of the Society of Friends played a prominent part in the development of corn-milling, brewing, pharmacy, and banking; and the Quaker families of the Darbys, Reynolds, Lloyds, and Huntsmans came to direct the destinies of the iron and steel industries at a period of rapid change. There were Baptists, like Thomas Newcomen, and Presbyterians, like James Watt, in engineering; independents, like John Roebuck and Joseph Dawson, alongside the Quakers, in iron-smelting; and Unitarians, including the M'Connels and the Gregs, in cotton-spinning. In cotton, moreover, the greatest inventor, Samuel Crompton, was a disciple of Emmanuel Swedenborg—who himself, it may be recalled, was an authority on metals and the technique of mines. Other industrialists, among whom were the Guests of South Wales, drew strength from the teaching of John Wesley. But Wesley's first appeal was to the poor and unprivileged, and the effects of Methodism are to be seen less in the quickening of enterprise than in the greater sobriety, diligence, and self-discipline of the workers who came under its influence.

Many explanations have been offered of this close association between industry and Dissent. It has been suggested that those who sought out new forms of worship would also naturally strike out new paths in secular fields. It has been argued that there is an intimate connection between the tenets peculiar to Nonconformity and the rules of conduct that lead to success in business. And it has been asserted that the exclusion of Dissenters from the universities, and from office in government and administration, forced many to seek an outlet for their abilities in industry and trade. There may be something in each of these contentions, but a simpler explanation lies in the fact that, broadly speaking, the Nonconformists constituted the better educated section of the middle classes. This view is supported by a consideration of the part played in the economic movement by the stream of energy that poured into England from Presbyterian Scotland after (though not immediately after) the Union of 1707. The greatest inventor of the age, James Watt, came from Scotland, as also did seven of his eight assistants in the business of erecting engines. Sir John Sinclair, Thomas Telford, John Macadam, David Mushet, and James Beaumont Neilson brought their Scottish vigour of mind and character to English agriculture, transport, and iron-making. Highlanders and Lowlanders, alike, tramped to the Lancashire cotton area, many of them pausing at the little village of Chowbent, where a fellow countryman named Cannan directed them to centres which offered scope for their several abilities. Among those who took the southern road to fortune in textiles were James McGuffog, James M'Connel, John Kennedy, George and Adam Murray, and——bearers of names that are honoured today, not only in Lancashire——John Gladstone and Henry Bannerman. These and other immigrants were not illiterate peasants. Some were sons of the manse, and even those of humbler station had been given at least the rudiments of a sound education in the village or burgh school of their native place.

If the Scottish system of primary education was in advance of that of any other European country at this time, the same was true of the Scottish universities. It was not from Oxford or Cambridge, where the torch burnt dim, but from Glasgow and Edinburgh, that the impulse to scientific inquiry and its practical application came. Many young men, attracted by the learning and personality of Joseph Black, Professor of

Chemistry at Glasgow and later at Edinburgh, were trained to methods of thought and experiment which were afterwards directed to industrial ends. Among them was James Keir, a pioneer in the chemical and glass industries, and (if the circle may be extended to those who were not formally students of Black, but owed much to his teaching and friendship) John Roebuck, James Watt, and Alexander Cochrane, the brilliant but unfortunate Earl of Dundonald.

In a humbler way the academies established by noncon-formist zeal for education—at Bristol, Manchester, Northamp-ton, Daventry, Warrington, and elsewhere—did for England in the eighteenth century something of what the universities did for Scotland. Open to all, irrespective of creed, they pro-vided a curriculum which, weighted, it is true, with Divinity, Rhetoric, and Jewish Antiquities, included Mathematics, His-tory, Geography, French, and Book-keeping. Among their pupils were Daniel Defoe (and a contemporary named Cruso), John Cope, John Howard, Thomas Malthus, and William Hazlitt—to name only a few of those who were to rise to distinc-tion in letters and public life. What is more to our immediate purpose, they were nurseries of scientific thought. Several of them were well equipped with 'philosophical instruments' and offered facilities for experiment: their teachers included men of the quality of Joseph Priestley and John Dalton; and from them proceeded a stream of future industrialists, among whom were John Roebuck (who was trained at Northampton before proceeding to Edinburgh and Leyden), Matthew Boulton, John Wilkinson, Benjamin Gott, and—of a later generation—Joseph Whitworth.

Apart from the dissenting academies, there were in many towns institutions which, like the national Society of Arts, were devoted to the improvement of methods of production. Infor-mal groups of scientists and manufacturers came into being in Lancashire and the Midlands, as well as at Edinburgh and Glasgow. Who can say how much the master cotton-spinners gained from their contact with Thomas Percival and John Dalton in the Literary and Philosophical Society of Manchester; or how much Birmingham and its province owe to the Lunar

Society, in which Erasmus Darwin, R. L. Edgeworth, Joseph Priestley, James Watt, Matthew Boulton, and Josiah Wedgwood brought their powerful minds to bear on the problems of life and, no less, on those of getting a living?

The conjuncture of growing supplies of land, labour, and capital made possible the expansion of industry; coal and steam provided the fuel and power for large-scale manufacture; low rates of interest, rising prices, and high expectations of profit offered the incentive. But behind and beyond these material and economic factors lay something more. Trade with foreign parts had widened men's views of the world, and science their conception of the universe: the industrial revolution was also a revolution of ideas. If it registered an advance in understanding of, and control over, Nature, it also saw the beginning of a new attitude to the problems of human society. And here, again, it was from Scotland, and the University of Glasgow in particular, that the clearest beam of light was thrown. It is, no doubt, an academic error to overstress the part played by speculative thought in shaping the lives of ordinary men and women: it is arguable that John Wesley, Tom Paine, William Cobbett, and Orator Hunt were of as much immediate consequence as David Hume, or even Jeremy Bentham. But, at least, there is one product of Scottish moral philosophy that cannot pass without mention in any account of the forces that produced the industrial revolution. The *Enquiry into the Nature and Causes of the Wealth of Nations,* which appeared in 1776, was to serve as a court of appeal on matters of economics and politics for generations to come. Its judgements were the material from which men not given to the study of treatises framed their maxims of conduct for business and government alike. It was under its influence that the idea of a more or less fixed volume of trade and employment, directed and regulated by the State, gave way—gradually and with many setbacks— to thoughts of unlimited progress in a free and expanding economy.

2
The Earlier Forms of Industry

IN the eighteenth century most of the people of Britain earned their living by work on the land. Conditions of life and labour varied with each small difference of configuration, sub-soil, and climate. But, apart from such diversities, there was one broad contrast that could hardly fail to impress itself on every traveller who rode through the English shires: that between the areas where the fields lay open, stretching unbroken to the horizon, and the areas where they were divided by quickset hedges, stone walls, fences, or rows of trees.

The open-field village, with its gradation of lord or squire, freeholders, copyholders, leaseholders, and cottagers, was well suited to the needs of a community producing grain and a small amount of livestock for its own subsistence. But, though it was more adaptable than has sometimes been supposed, it tended to hold by the methods of cultivation and economic relations of the past. Before a system of drainage or a new rotation of crops could be introduced it was necessary to win the assent of a body of men most of whom were satisfied with customary practice and suspicious of change. Progress in agriculture was bound up with the creation of new units of administration in which the individual had more scope for experiment; and this meant the parcelling out and enclosure of the common fields, or the breaking up of the rough pasture and waste which had previously contributed little to the output of the village.

Enclosure had been taking place almost continuously from at least as early as the thirteenth century. Its development had been connected with production, not for subsistence, but for the market. In Tudor and Stuart times much of it had been for the purpose of supplying wool to the expanding textile industry; and, even in the half-century after 1700, the enclosures were most often in regions specially suited to pasture. It was the growing demand for wool and leather, rather than for grain, that provided the incentive.

The process was closely associated with the concentration of ownership into fewer hands. It was not that there was any pressing need for larger farms: many of the holdings in the open fields were quite big enough to be efficient units of production. But when a single lord, or a few substantial squires, came to control an area it was easy to bring about changes of method, whether on a compact home farm, or indirectly through conditions imposed on the leaseholders, who were coming to take the place of the freeholders or customary tenants of the older system.

Many of the earlier enclosures had been carried out by men who had made their fortunes in trade or in government service and who sought the prestige that, in England, has always gone with the possession of the soil. But in the first half of the eighteenth century the old landed aristocracy, which had lost much in the Civil Wars, was reasserting its claims to its former place in society. Noblemen were making much use of entail, so as to keep their properties intact. Encouraged by low rates of interest, they were mortgaging their estates and using the proceeds to buy more land. Above all, they were initiating enclosures. Most of these were made by private arrangements between the proprietors concerned: they took place in parishes where the number of owners was small and the average holding correspondingly large, and these were generally the ones in which pasture was a prominent activity. Where the land was in many hands it was often necessary to buy out the freeholders: the disappearance of the yeoman, about which much has been written, was not generally a result of the enclosure but a prelude to it. If the freeholders proved obdurate it was possible to obtain Parliamentary powers to give effect to the wishes of those, however few in number, who controlled the greater part of the soil. But enclosure by Act did not play an important part until after 1760: many of the yeomen seem to have been willing to sell their small freeholds and to use the money to set up as large leasehold farmers; and some (there can be little doubt) transferred their capital and energies to manufacture.

There were, however, humbler classes of people who received little or no consideration. The cottagers, who had cultivated a few strips in the open fields, and supplemented their incomes by part-time work on those of their wealthier neighbours, might, indeed, be given a small holding when the land was re-divided. But it was less easy to graze a cow, keep fowls, or gather fuel, when the greater part of the waste had been allotted to the squire or the larger cultivators. On the fringe of most open-field villages, there were many squatters who obtained a precarious living, either by primitive husbandry on tiny intakes, or by wage-earning, poaching, begging, thieving, or the receipt of poor relief. Taking little part in the life of the community, they had been tolerated by the easy-going, open-field cultivators. But the enclosed village had little use for such people: their presence was an obstacle to the full utilization of the land, and their poverty laid a burden of parish rates on the tenant farmers. Evicted from their cottages, which were afterwards razed to the ground, they crowded to areas where the fields were still open, or took to vagrancy. They and their descendants must have contributed largely to the body of semi-employed, inefficient labour that was to trouble the peace of politicians and poor-law administrators until 1834, and beyond.

Some writers who have dwelt at length on the fate of those who were forced to leave the land have tended to overlook the constructive activities that were being carried on inside the fences. The essential fact about enclosure is that it brought about an increase in the productivity of the soil. There has been much discussion as to whether it led to a decline in the number of cultivators, and some who hold that it did write as though this were a consequence to be deplored. It is a truism, however, that the standard of life of a nation is raised when fewer people are needed to provide the means of subsistence. Many of those who were divorced from the soil (as the stereotyped phrase goes) were free to devote themselves to other activities: it was precisely because enclosure released (or drove) men from the land that it is to be counted among the processes that led to the industrial revolution, with the higher standards of consumption this brought with it.

The enclosures were initiated by 'spirited landowners' many of whom adhered to some particular school of agricultural doctrine or practice. Among the most celebrated of the reformers was Jethro Tull (1674–1741), a law student who, at the age of twenty-five, took to farming with considerable success. Tull held to a peculiar theory of cultivation. Believing that plants could obtain nutriment only in the form of tiny particles, which he called atoms, he advocated a constant pulverization of the soil by deep working; and to facilitate this he invented, or developed, in 1714, a horse-drawn hoe. In many respects his teaching was retrograde. He was an opponent of the use of manures. His practice of sowing in drills, wide apart, was economical of seed, but wasteful of land. And his hostility to rotation (supported as it was by a claim to have grown wheat for thirteen successive years on the same land) set back the movement to progressive farming in many parts of England. Tull was a crank, and his importance in the history of agriculture has been vastly exaggerated. It was not from his farms in Berkshire, but from those of the large-scale proprietors of Norfolk, that the real innovations came.

What is known as the Norfolk system was (as an American, Naomi Riches, has said) a series of interrelated technical, economic and legal processes, combined on an enclosed farm. It included the introduction to sandy soils of marl and clay, the rotation of crops, the growing of turnips, clover, and new grasses, the production of grain and cattle rather than of sheep, and cultivation by tenants, under long leases, on large-scale holdings. Some of its features were derived from Continental example; for Norfolk, with its textile and fishing trades, had close connections with the Netherlands. But most of them were the product of an indigenous race of energetic landlords and cultivators. Lord Lovell (1697–1755), predecessor and relative of the famous Coke of Holkham, was active in the use of marls, the draining of marshes, and the practice of rotation; and the name of Viscount Townshend (1674–1738) has been connected with the introduction of the turnip as a field crop, though recent research has shown that he was the popularizer, rather than the originator of this. But the Norfolk system, like every major innovation, was the work of many hands and brains. Much of the history of agriculture in the eighteenth century is concerned with the spread to other parts of Britain of its four-course rotation (turnips, barley, clover, wheat, or some variant of this) in place of the three-course (winter crop, spring crop, and fallow) of the old Midlands system. The cultivation of grasses and turnips meant that areas of what had been permanent pasture could be brought under the plough; and, since cattle could now be maintained through the winter, the supply of natural fertilizer for the cereal and root crops was increased. But the transition to 'convertible husbandry' was very slow: the open-field system, with its concentration on grain rather than livestock, died hard. In no part of Britain—not even in Norfolk itself—were the innovations adopted on such a scale as to make it possible to speak of an agricultural, or an agrarian, revolution.

In all parts of the world textiles have been one of the earliest offshoots of a peasant economy. In Britain wool from the backs of sheep had, for many generations, provided the material for an activity second only to agriculture in the number of people it employed and the volume of trade it supported. The importance of this industry in the eyes of government is attested by a long list of measures which sought to prevent the export of raw wool, the emigration of skilled workers, and the import of fabrics that might compete with woollen cloths in the home market. People were exhorted, or constrained, to dress in English materials, and even the dead were not allowed to be buried in any fabric other than wool.

Production consisted of a long chain of processes. First the wool was sorted, cleaned, and sometimes dyed. Next it was either combed, to separate the long hairs from the short, or carded, to make a fleecy roll with the fibres lying roughly parallel. After this it was spun, woven, fulled, washed, tentered (or stretched), bleached, dressed, and sheared. These processes called for different degrees of skill and strength: women and children could do the sorting, cleaning, and spinning, but combing, weaving, and the later operations were men's work. Some of them were performed with the aid of simple apparatus in the home. But fulling (in which the cloth was treated with fuller's earth and beaten with heavy hammers to mat the texture) was conducted in mills worked by horses or water power; dressing, or raising the nap, was done in gig mills; and dyeing needed vats and other equipment too large to be housed in a cottage.

There was probably no county of England and Wales in which woollen cloth was not produced by the part-time work of peasants, farmers, and agricultural labourers. But there were areas of concentration in the West Country, East Anglia, and Yorkshire, where men and women had become specialist spinners or weavers, thinking first of wool, treating work on the land as, at most, a by-occupation, and making yarn and cloth far superior to anything that could be produced by the rough-handed peasant.

The organization of the industry was complex, and varied from place to place. In the West Country the well-to-do clothier gave out wool to carders and spinners, and yarn to weavers, all of whom worked in their own homes; and the undressed cloth was then passed to fullers, dressers, and shearmen, who finished it in small mills or workshops under his supervision. In East Anglia there were master-combers who controlled the work of the spinners and weavers, and merchants who directed that of the finishers. In the West Riding the clothier was often a man of quite small capital, who, aided by his family and a few apprentices or journeymen, himself wove cloth in a workshop attached to his home, using yarn spun by women in the cottages. But there were also wealthy worsted manufacturers here who gave out work by the piece to spinners, weavers, and others who worked for wages. Some clothiers sold their wares direct to merchants or to customers abroad; some disposed of them through factors at Blackwell Hall in London; some took them to the annual Sturbridge Fair at Cambridge; and the Yorkshire clothier-weavers carried their undressed webs to weekly markets held at Halifax, Wakefield, Leeds, and Bradford.

Other branches of textiles depended for their raw materials partly, at least, on foreign sources of supply. Raw silk and organzine (thrown silk) were brought from China, Italy, Spain, and Turkey, flax from Ireland, the Baltic and North America, and cotton from the Levant and the West Indies. The manufacture of these was carried on under conditions similar in essentials to those in the woollen industry. The silk weavers tended to concentrate in towns, at Spitalfields, Coventry, Norwich, and Macclesfield. They worked in garrets or sheds in each of which perhaps half a dozen looms were controlled by a capitalist employer. The manufacture of linen and cotton was more widely scattered, but there was a strong tendency to localization in Lancashire and the Lowlands of Scotland. Cotton was too short in staple to be used as warp, except in the production of small fabrics, such as handkerchiefs: hence what was later to become by far the greatest centre of textile production had to depend for its yarn largely on linen and wool, and only to a less extent on cotton. The typical products of Lancashire in the first half of the eighteenth century were pure woollens, cotton-linen fustians and checks, and smallwares (including tapes, braid, ribbons, incles, and thread) made of such diverse materials as cotton, linen, silk, worsted, and mohair.

The organization of the textile manufactures of Lancashire cannot be described in a few words. Suffice it to say that the central figure was a merchant, clothier, or linen-draper, who employed putters-out to distribute material, either direct to the scattered spinners and weavers, or to country manufacturers who, in turn, put it out in their own areas. There were some farmer-weavers, who divided their energies between the plough and the loom. But most of the weavers, even in the country, were virtually full-time operatives; and in the larger towns, like

Manchester, where smallwares were produced on expensive Dutch looms, the workers were entirely dependent on the capital of the merchants and linen-drapers who not only provided the material, but often owned the bleach-crofts, dye-houses and workshops where the finishing processes were performed.

The clothing, as distinct from the textile, trades were relatively small and unimportant, for most families made their own garments or employed seamstresses who worked for wretchedly low wages. Beaver hats had long been made in London; felt hats, of rabbit skin and other material, were produced at many places, including Stockport and Manchester; and straw plaiting and straw hat-making gave rise to a cottage industry, conducted mainly by women and children in their own homes, in Bedfordshire, Buckinghamshire, and Hertfordshire. Stockings were still knitted by hand in cottages, especially in Scotland and Wales, where there were fairs specialized to their sale; but from the days of Elizabeth, when a cleric, William Lee, had invented a stocking-frame, many men, women, and children in London had found employment in frame-work knitting. In the early eighteenth century the industry was moving from the metropolis to the counties of Derby, Nottingham, and Leicester, where control by the Framework Knitters' Company was ineffective, and where labour was cheap. The hosier, who owned the frames, usually kept a few at his own shop or warehouse, but most of them were hired to knitters who worked in their homes, on yarn of varied materials brought to their doors by putters-out. Before the middle of the century there were Midland hosiers who owned as many as a hundred frames, and a new class of master-stockingers had begun to act as intermediaries between them and the knitters. Originally putters-out, these men entered into contracts with the hosiers for work which they gave out at piece-rates, and also hired frames which they sub-let, at increased rents, to the knitters. Though the hosier continued to own both the material and the frames, he had become little more than a merchant, without direct relations with those who depended on him for employment.

Even in the first half of the eighteenth century, however, there were portents of change in the textile industries. Here and there, for technical reasons, small groups of men were being brought together into workshops and little water-driven mills. There was much innovation and experiment. In 1717 Thomas Lombe, whose brother had brought designs of machines from Italy, set up a true factory on the River Derwent, where nearly 300 workers were employed in throwing silk. It was the precursor of a host of similar factories—though of few in silk manufacture, which has never, indeed, found Britain congenial to its growth. In 1733 a Lancashire clock-maker, John Kay, made a simple, but important, improvement in the loom, by which the shuttle, mounted on wheels, was struck by hammers and so driven through the warp. The fly-shuttle was a labour-saving device: it enabled a single weaver, sitting at the loom and holding in his hand strings attached to the hammers, to make cloth of a width that had previously required the work of two men. But the device encountered opposition from the Lancashire weavers, and there were probably mechanical difficulties that were only slowly overcome: it was not until after 1760 that the fly-shuttle came into general use. In 1738 Lewis Paul of Birmingham, the son of a physician, hit on an idea which was to do for spinning what Kay's device was ultimately to do for weaving. The carded cotton or wool was passed through two sets of rollers revolving at different speeds, and in this way was drawn out before it passed to the spindle which gave the twist. But attempts to make use of the contrivance in small mills at Birmingham, London, Northampton, and Leominster all failed, partly, it would appear, because of technical defects, but also perhaps (as Paul said) because of the poor quality and shiftless habits of the workers. It was not until nearly two generations later, when Arkwright took up the idea, that roller spinning was able to transform the methods of producing yarn, and so virtually to create an industry based solely on cotton, and conducted in factories.

The other leading industries of Britain were all, like textiles, in one way or another, closely connected with agriculture. This was true, in particular, of the mining of coal. It was the owners of the land who controlled the working of the underground seams and drew from them their rents and royalties. Coal-mining was carried on in a rural rather than an urban setting: it made use of large numbers of horses for winding and trans-port, and to maintain these most colliery owners kept farms on which they grew oats and other crops. The colliers them-selves were close to the soil: it was usual for them to leave the pits for work on the land in the months of harvest; and the methods of hiring, and relations with employers, were very similar to those of the agricultural labourer.

At the beginning of the eighteenth century most of the coal-fields had long passed the stage of outcrop, or pit-and-adit mining. Shafts were sunk, sometimes to a depth of 200 feet or more; underground galleries were extensive; and primitive systems of ventilation had been devised. Access by sea to the London market made the Northumberland and Durham coal-field by far the largest and best developed area of production. Here landed proprietors and other capitalists formed partner-ships or companies, employed expert 'viewers' to give advice on the conduct of their operations, and appointed overmen at the separate pits to control the undermen who supervised the work of the hewers and barrowmen. In most other coal-fields there was no such hierarchy of officials: the working colliers formed themselves into companies, of six or eight or a dozen men, and made contracts through their leader (a charter-master or butty) either to work the whole of a small pit, to get and carry to the customer a certain amount of coal, or to drive a certain length of underground way for an agreed sum.

This difference of organization was associated with a differ-ence in the manner of working the coal. In Northumberland and Durham, Cumberland, Lancashire, and Scotland, the method was that of the pillar and stall: the stall or bord in which the pitman hewed, assisted by a single boy, was sup-ported by columns of coal; and as much as a half, or even two-thirds, of the mineral might be left unworked to support the roof. But in the Midlands—in Shropshire, Staffordshire, and Warwickshire—where roofs and floors were stronger, the colliers worked co-operatively by longwall, supporting the roof with props, and flinging the stone or slack behind them into the goaf from which the coal had already been worked.

There were differences also in the methods of moving the coal underground. In the northern field of England this was done by barrowmen, who dragged wooden sledges, shod with runners of ash, from the coal face to the pit bottom; but by 1750 ponies, tended by boys, were beginning to replace the men in the Newcastle area. In other places the coal was carried in baskets by youths or women; and in Fifeshire the wives and daughters of the colliers went bent under heavy loads, bearing the coal, not only along the underground passages, but by a series of ladders up the shaft to the surface. What a nineteenth-century colliery owner called 'the repugnant mode of conveying coals on the backs of ladies' continued in some districts till as late as 1842.

The chief technical problems of getting coal arose from the presence in the pits of gas and water. The inert gas, chokedamp, might be dispersed by dragging bunches of furze along the galleries, or by other simple devices. But the inflammable firedamp was a more serious matter. It was sometimes dealt with by a fireman, who, clad in leather or wet rags, carried a long pole with a lighted candle at the end, with which, at some personal risk, he exploded the gas. In the larger mines of the Newcastle area in the 1730s it was the practice to sink two shafts: an iron basket of flaming coals, suspended in one of these, caused the gas-laden air to rise, and so drew fresh supplies from the surface down the other shaft. About the same time, to avoid the danger of working by the light of candles, a device, known as the steel-mill, was introduced into the Cumberland and Tyneside mines. A boy, standing by the hewer, caused a small toothed wheel to revolve against a flint, and so produced a shower of sparks, sufficient to give a dim illumination. But the use of the steel-mill was no guarantee against accidents, and at some pits the men preferred to make shift with such light as they could get from putrefying fish or pieces of phosphorescent wood.

Water presented the mining engineer or viewer with an even more intractable problem. In the northern coalfield it was the practice to line the shaft with sheepskins, covered with wooden 'tubbing', to keep back the springs that would otherwise have made it impossible to sink through the wet strata. The water that drained from the workings into the sump at the pit bottom was raised to the surface by a variety of devices, including hand-pumps and the 'endless-chain' of pots, worked by men, donkeys, or, occasionally, water-wheels or windmills. The cost of drainage was great and the incentive to find more efficient methods of removing water from the pits correspondingly strong. It was probably the needs of the metal miners of Cornwall that led Thomas Savery to devise in 1698 a pumping engine which involved the use of steam. Erected in a recess in the pit shaft, this consisted simply of a boiler and a condenser fitted with pipes, one of which ran down the shaft to the sump and the other to the surface. The vacuum created by condensation of the steam sucked the water from the sump; and injection of fresh steam from the boiler forced it up the eduction pipe to ground level. But the waste of energy involved in bringing steam into direct contact with cold water was enormous. It was to avoid this that an ironmonger of Dartmouth, Thomas Newcomen (1663–1729), invented, in 1708, an entirely different form of self-acting atmospheric engine. A great beam of timber, pivoted high above the ground on a solid piece of masonry, was given freedom to swing vertically through the arc of a circle. At one end the beam was connected to a piston which moved up and down, as steam was first injected, and then condensed, in the cylinder. These movements were transmitted to the beam, and so to the pump rods attached to its other end, by movement of which the water was drawn up a pipe in the mine shaft. Many modifications and additions were made by Newcomen and his successors. First employed at collieries in the Midlands, the contrivance was soon adopted in the northern coalfield, and by 1765 there were about 100 engines at work in the neighbourhood of the Tyne and Wear. They made possible the working of seams in and below the watery layers, and so were an important factor in increasing the output of the mines. Thomas Newcomen deserves a very special place in the gallery of the pioneers of modern technology.

The engine was a device used solely for pumping: it could

not be employed in the process of winding. This was done by horse gins which drew the hazel corves, or baskets, containing the coal, to the top of the shaft. Sometimes the colliers ascended or descended in the baskets; but more often they thrust a leg through a loop in the winding rope, and, clustered together, rode the shaft, the boys sitting on the knees of the men, or simply clinging to the rope with hands and feet. Accidents, by striking the walls, or falling to the bottom of the shaft, were not infrequent.

The limits of output were set by difficulties of transport, not only underground for the individual pit, but also, on the surface, for the industry as a whole. In the North there were wagon ways, with wooden rails, from the collieries to the rivers, and about a thousand sea-going vessels of 300 or 400 tons carried the coal to distant parts. But the inland fields had to rely on transport in panniers, slung across the backs of horses, or in wagons moving along the ill-made roads. Not until better highways and canals came in could the market be more than local.

The getting of coal offered little opportunity for the application of mechanical devices in hewing and underground carriage: the struggle to wrest coal from the earth was very much a soldiers' battle, from which swift results are not to be expected. Estimates of production for early periods can be little better than guesses. But it seems likely that the output was about $2\frac{1}{2}$ million tons a year in 1700, and $4\frac{3}{4}$ million tons in 1750. Such figures are small compared with the round 10 million of 1800, the 16 million of 1829, and the far larger tonnages that were to follow: it was the nineteenth, rather than the eighteenth, century that was the age of coal. But, even in 1700 and 1750, fuel was basic to the development of most processes of production, and the relatively slow rate of progress in coal-mining set limits to the expansion of British industry in general.

One of the industries that made much use of fuel was the smelting and 'fining' of iron. In this case, however, the fuel was not coal, but charcoal, and here again there was close connection with the land, through the proprietors of the woods and coppices where it was produced. It was the presence of trees, rather than of iron ore, that determined the location of iron-works, for it was cheaper to move ore than wood or charcoal over long distances. In the sixteenth and seventeenth centuries a thriving iron industry had grown up in the Weald of Sussex and Kent. But the exhaustion of the forests in this region (largely because of the demands of ship-building, as well as of iron-making) had led to a decline; and by 1700 the industry was moving away to other parts of the country where woodlands still remained or new coppices could be planted.

To produce iron, the ore had first to be smelted in a blast furnace, and the molten metal run into pigs. It could then be either re-melted in a small air furnace and turned into castings, or passed to the forges where it was heated and hammered into bars of wrought iron. These in turn were sent to the slitting mills, where they were heated, passed through grooved rollers, and so drawn out and cut into rods. Cast iron was hard, but brittle; it was the material for such things as domestic pots and pans, and—a use by no means negligible in a century of many wars—some forms of ordnance. Wrought iron, with its lower carbon content, was malleable, tensile, and able to withstand strain: it was used for making horseshoes, nails, picks and spades, locks and bolts, wire, and tools of all kinds.

Furnaces, forges, and slitting mills were generally separate undertakings—often, because of the limited supplies of fuel, carried on at a distance one from another, by producers independent of each other. The outstanding innovation in iron production in the early eighteenth century was the substitution of coke for charcoal in the production of pig iron and castings. For more than a century one projector after another had sought for a way of effecting this, and several patents had been taken out. These, however, represented aspirations, rather than achievements, for the sulphur in the coke was responsible for a product which was unfit for castings and which, when turned into wrought iron, was so brittle as to be unusable. It was not until 1709 that a Quaker ironmaster, Abraham Darby of Coal-brookdale in Shropshire, managed to produce pig iron of quality, smelted with coke. His furnace seems to have been of the height usual in the charcoal-iron industry, and his bellows were not exceptionally powerful. The explanation of his success almost certainly lay in the clod coal, close at hand, which, with its low content of sulphur, produced a coke, unlike that from the coal of other areas, suitable for the purpose of the blast furnace. Darby's discovery was to lead to results of great importance to the future of Britain as an industrial nation, but the full fruits came only later in the century. The use of the process spread slowly—for long only within the circle of Darby's family and friends. Quaker reticence—and possibly a desire to keep the knowledge from competitors—may have had something to do with this, but the uses to which the coke-smelted pig could be put were, in any case, restricted. Darby's iron was, or was considered to be, too impure to serve as material for the forge-master: it was only in the production of castings that mineral fuel was able to replace charcoal.

The discovery led to a slow growth of furnaces and foundries on the coalfields, rather than in the neighbourhood of the forests. It enabled the millwrights to get better materials for some of their purposes, and led to a substitution of cast for wrought iron in some commodities of common use. These results were not unimportant. But they left the greater part of the iron industry still in its semi-rural setting, bound for its power to the falling stream, and for its fuel to the shrinking woodlands.

Intermediate in carbon content between cast iron, on the one hand, and wrought iron, on the other, is steel. This was made by putting pieces of wrought iron, covered with charcoal, into an oven and keeping them at a high temperature for several days. The blister steel that resulted was then cut into small gadds, bound together in faggots, re-heated in a furnace, and forged into shear steel. Probably because the raw material was iron of high quality, imported from Sweden, the making of steel was localized about Newcastle upon Tyne. Costs of production were great, and the use of steel was confined to the making of cutlery, razors, the better kinds of edge-tools, swords, guns, and the working parts of clocks and watches. In the early 1740s, a Quaker clockmaker of Sheffield, Benjamin Huntsman, devised a process of melting blister or shear steel in small crucibles, and so obtained a purer and more uniform product. His cast steel was to play a leading part in the growth of many industries, including engineering. But, as with others of these early discoveries, knowledge of the process spread slowly, and it was not until towards the end of the century that crucible steel came into extensive use.

In the manufacture, as distinct from the production, of iron it was possible to make full use of mineral fuel, and it was, therefore, on the coalfields that the makers of tools and agricultural implements, chains, locks and bolts, and, above all, nails, tended to congregate. The largest single area of production was in south Staffordshire and north-east Worcestershire, especially along the valleys of the Tame and Stour, where many old corn mills had been converted to the slitting of iron. An early concentration on the making of saddlery had, apparently, given rise to the production of bits, stirrups, and other iron-work connected with horses at Walsall and West Bromwich; and Birmingham had already begun to specialize in the making of guns, swords, and those varied lighter wares of metal for which she was to become famous. But in the countryside, about these towns, the chief activity was the making of nails, for which the American colonies (where the houses were built of wood) provided a large and expanding market.

There was localization of the metal-working industries also in South Yorkshire and the neighbouring parts of Derbyshire: Sheffield concentrated on the best qualities of cutlery and tools, and the villages round about were engaged in the less skilled work of making scythes, sickles, and nails. At Newcastle upon Tyne, again, there were many cutlers, and nearby at Swalwell and Winlaton, Ambrose Crowley, who had come there from Stourbridge, set up a highly paternalistic enterprise for the production of anchors, chains, tools, and nails. At Winlaton the smiths and other master-workmen had their shops in a square, erected by Crowley, where they lived under semi-collegiate conditions, with their own chaplain, surgeon, and schoolmaster, and their own sick and superannuation fund. Such circumstances, however, were exceptional. In the West Midlands, in South Yorkshire, and in West Lancashire (where there was also a development of ironworking in the countryside between Liverpool, Wigan, and Warrington) production was carried on in small shops or sheds attached to the scattered homes of the workers. Ironmongers gave out rods at their warehouses and the nailmakers and others brought back their finished product. But, at a later stage, there grew up a body of factors or foggers who performed functions similar to those of the putter-out in Lancashire or the stockinger or bagman in the East Midlands.

Iron and steel do not lend themselves so readily as textile fibres to machine methods: there was innovation in the types of product, but little in the processes of manufacture. The number of workers increased, and there was some growth of specialization. But the limits of output were set by those of the raw material; and it was not until late in the century, when it became possible to produce wrought iron with coal, that there could be any spectacular expansion of the metal-working trades.

Large-scale production required not only division of labour and specialized appliances, but also the support of an organized system of transport, commerce, and credit. According to all contemporary observers, the internal communications of Britain were far from meeting the needs of the industrialists. The roads of England, depending as they did for construction and repair on amateur surveyors and unskilled statute labour, were mostly unsuited to wheeled traffic; and an important means of land carriage was by pack-horses, which travelled, sometimes 100 or more in line, on stone causeways laid alongside, or in the middle of, the highways. When enclosures were made the opportunity was taken to widen and straighten the approaches to the villages, and in some areas turnpikes were constructed by trusts which, under an Act of 1662, were empowered to raise capital on the security of their future revenue from tolls. But there was much opposition to what was in fact an enclosure of the highroads, and the toll-bars were often broken down. It was not until after the middle of the century that the turnpike roads provided an efficient channel of communication in areas at all remote from London.

For bulky, heavy, or fragile goods, the rivers and seas afforded a far cheaper and safer means of carriage. An extensive coasting trade was carried on between ports, the number of which ran into scores. Some of these, like Newcastle, Hull, and Bristol, already large, were to extend their trade enormously as time went on; others, like Whitby, Scarborough, King's Lynn, and Yarmouth, were to fall behind as the forces of the industrial revolution brought a concentration of trade hardly less intense than that of industry. Many, though not all, were situated at the mouths of navigable rivers, which, like the highways of the sea, played an important part in developing the inter-regional trade (and hence the localization of industry), which was a marked feature of the English economy in the period 1700–60. Nearly the whole of the fuel and most of the food of Londoners came to them by water: coal was loaded into keels on the Tyne, and transferred to sea-going colliers which carried it to the Pool, where it was unloaded into lighters; and grain and other produce of the Thames Valley were brought down the river in barges. On the Severn, trows laden with coal, hollow-ware, and nails from Shropshire and Worcestershire were floated down to Bristol, and dragged back upstream, with their cargoes of bar iron, clay, and West Indian produce, by gangs of powerful (but short-lived) bow-hauliers. The smaller rivers were less navigable. Some of them were obstructed by weirs and fish-garths; there were many shallows which, in times of drought, impeded navigation; and the unsocial practice of throwing ballast overboard in an attempt to float over these sometimes put an end to traffic. Enlightened landowners and industrialists, especially in the North, formed companies and obtained statutory powers to widen and deepen many of the waterways. At an early date the improvement of the Salwarpe had aided the rise of Droitwich as a centre of salt production; but a later development of the Weaver led to a much more rapid growth of the Cheshire 'wiches'. The deepening of the Aire and Calder made it possible to bring to the West Riding the long-stapled wools of Lincoln and Leicestershire; and that of the Don stimulated the growth of the metal trades of Rotherham and, later, of Sheffield. In Lancashire there was

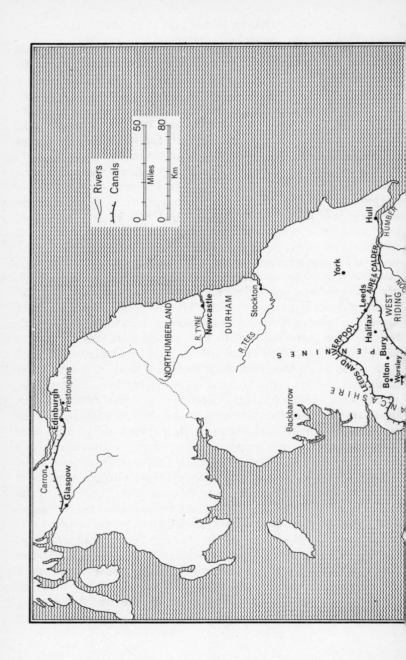

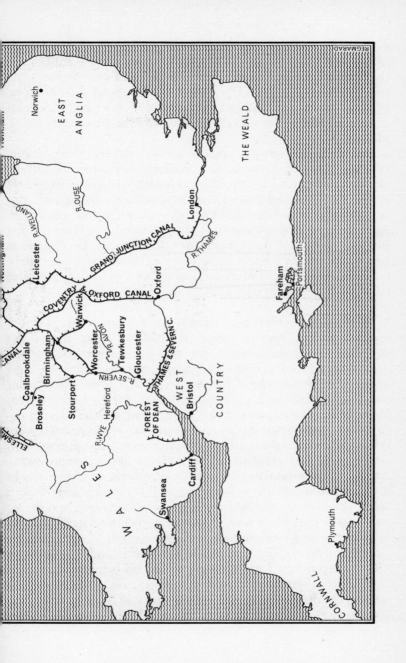

exceptional activity: the Douglas navigation enabled the coals of the pits about Wigan to reach the estuary of the Ribble and the Fylde; the successive improvements of the Mersey and Irwell played a part in the growth of Liverpool as a port, and of Manchester as a centre of textile manufacture; and the canalization of the little Sankey Brook brought prosperity to St. Helens and Warrington.

But there was much opposition to each of these undertakings, from landowners who objected to the diversion of the streams, from traders of old-established river ports like York, Gainsborough, and Bawtry, and from all who disliked the idea of paying tolls on what had been thought of as free waterways. At their best, English rivers could provide but a slow and expensive means of transport. The use of them, no longer as highways, but as feeders for a more efficient system of canals, was among the most important of the innovations of the later decades of the century.

Internal trade was conducted by merchants most of whom specialized in a narrow range of products. Some themselves travelled about the country, but many employed 'riders-out' to secure orders and collect payment from customers. In overseas trade the merchant was a specialist, not in a particular commodity, but in a particular market. He had long ceased to voyage with his wares, which were now entrusted to a supercargo or dispatched to an agent abroad. Though ships were relatively small, the costs of construction, equipment, and repair were too great to be borne by a single person: many merchants, manufacturers, master mariners, and others held a fourth, a sixteenth, a thirty-second, or even a sixty-fourth share in what was in effect a joint-stock enterprise; and in this way a large part of the well-to-do came to take an active interest in coastwise and foreign trade.

Britain was self-supporting in foodstuffs and, on balance, was an exporter of grain. But she leaned heavily on foreign countries for timber, bar iron, hemp, and other materials needed for the building and maintenance of her ships; for silk, cotton, and dyestuffs used in the textile industries; and for sugar, rum, tea, coffee, and tobacco, as well as for many finished products. In return Britain exported manufactured goods of all kinds, but especially those made of wool, iron, and leather. Cloth, firearms, hardware, and trinkets were sent to Africa and exchanged for slaves, who were shipped to the West Indies to pay for the luxuries and raw material which constituted the final cargo in this disreputable, triangular trade.

Historians have tended to pay undue attention to the commerce with distant lands. The overwhelming bulk of the import and export trade was with the Continent and, in particular, with the countries nearest to Britain. Compared with this, the traffic with India, the West Indies, and North America was small, and that with Africa insignificant. The fortunes made by members of the East India and Africa Companies must not be allowed to hide the fact that it was not the monopolistic organizations, trafficking in silver and slaves, but individual merchants—of London, the out-ports, and scores of inland towns—dealing in wares of common use, that built up British commerce at this time. Trade with the Baltic, from which Britain drew her naval stores, was of more political and economic consequence than that with the whole of the tropics.

II

In this highly condensed account of the chief activities that were to figure in the industrial revolution there are many omissions. Lack of space (and in some cases lack of knowledge) precludes a description of the builders and shipwrights, fishermen and sailors, tanners and leathermakers, papermakers and printers, and many others. It is unlikely, however, that a study of these would modify in any important respect the outline of the picture that has been presented.

Industry was rural rather than urban. In the two preceding centuries it had moved away from the towns to the countryside, partly to escape from municipal and gild restrictions, partly for technical reasons. Dependence on the sea for the carriage of goods led to a greater peopling of the coastal, than of the inland, regions; and the importance of transport by river was reflected in a thickening of population along the valleys of the Thames, Severn, and Clyde. There was concentration on the flanks of the Pennines, the Cotswolds, the Devonshire moors, and the uplands of southern Scotland, all of which were sources, not only of wool, but of the soft water needed for several of the processes of what was still the staple British industry. Corn mills, fulling mills, furnaces, forges, slitting mills, and cutlery and tool-grinding works depended on falling water for their power. Few towns (Sheffield was one of the few) had supplies of water sufficient to maintain many such plants, and in any case the ironworks needed to be near the woodlands, and the metal trades near the coal mines, which provided the fuel. The distribution of natural resources, and especially that of water, led to a wide geographical spread of population.

There were, it is true, towns of substantial size—seaports, river ports, and marketing centres. London, with its shipyards, warehouses, breweries and distilleries, and its varied crafts producing consumers' goods (silks and leather-ware, furniture, clocks and watches, glass, pottery, cutlery, and jewellery) occupied an even more important place in the economic life of the nation than it does today. But it owed this development to its position as a capital city and a port; and the aggregation of population in London and the neighbouring parts of Middlesex, Surrey, and Kent was originally less the result of manufacture than of trade—as was also that of other large towns, like Bristol, Norwich, and Glasgow.

Industries were migratory (which is not to say that the workers and entrepreneurs themselves migrated). Iron production was transferred from the Weald to the West Midlands, silk and hosiery from London to East Anglia, the Midlands, and the North; and salt-making from the coast of Durham to the plains of Cheshire. The structure of industry was flexible. The textile, clothing, hardware, and many other trades were carried on under what the text-books call the domestic system of industry—a phrase, convenient indeed, but misleading, for the chief characteristic of these trades is that they conformed to no single system of organization. Men of different degrees of skill, capital, and ability to bear risks could find in them full scope for their endowments, and there was a wide, almost a bewildering, variety of forms. The same was true, though in a less degree, of mining and iron-making. Two or three partners, with very little capital, could open a pit or erect a forge, and compete, not unsuccessfully, with great enterprises like those of the Grand Allies of the Tyne or the Quaker dynasties of Shropshire. Since processes were relatively simple men and women moved easily from one occupation to another: there was much coming and going between manufacture and agriculture; and mines, furnaces, and cottage workshops suspended their activities in the summer and early autumn so that the workers could help with the harvests. Most of the capital was embodied, not in buildings and machines, but in stocks of material in process of production: resources could be transferred readily from industry to trade, or from trade to industry; and a man might describe himself at one time as a master manufacturer and at another as a merchant. Since combinations of workers were few and weak, it was not difficult to substitute capital for labour, or one kind of labour for another; and the specialization of factors of production, which is the prerequisite of a lowering of costs, could proceed with little or no restraint.

In such respects industry, in the period 1700–60, conformed closely to the models constructed by economists a century or more later. There is a danger, however, of overstressing the social advantages of the scheme of things, and, in particular, of idealizing the conditions of labour. It is doubtful whether the union of manufacture and agriculture was altogether a happy one for the worker, for it meant that his hands became roughened and gnarled in a way that confined his work—in textiles especially—to the coarser types of product. It is true that most workers enjoyed whatever advantages may be supposed to attach to ownership of their tools and appliances. But the acquisition of a pick and shovel, an anvil and hammer, or a set of saws and files was almost always the occasion of a debt. There could be little comfort in a cottage in which the principal piece of furniture was a loom or a knitting frame, and in which the atmosphere was heavy with fluff and dust, or with fumes from the charcoal stoves used in wool-combing and many other operations. It is true, again, that most workers were free in some measure to determine their hours of work and play. In mining absenteeism seems to have been at least as common as it is today, and holidays were numerous and well observed. Many domestic workers were accustomed to give Sunday, Monday, and sometimes Tuesday, to idleness or sport. This meant, however, that they had to work long into the night for the rest of the week; and though the irregularity was not, perhaps, of much consequence for the adult (some writers of books behave in much the same way) it can hardly have been good for the children who helped him.

Relations between employers and workers are generally best when they are direct. In agriculture many labourers were servants who lived in, though there was a growing tendency for them to set up homes of their own. But in industries in which the workers were scattered over a wide area, and in which (as in the manufacture of cotton and wool) a man might give employment to 2,000 or 3,000 people, personal contact was impossible. The closest ties were those among members of the group who worked together: in mining and fishing the 'company', in glass-making the 'chair', and in most cases the family. But the fact that men, women, and children worked side by side does not imply that the household was a self-contained unit: no woman could spin the quantity (or variety) of yarn that her husband required, for technique was such that the full-time work of five or six spinners was needed to keep a single loom in operation. The intermediary saved the weaver from having to go to and fro in search of yarn, but he tended to drive hard bargains: in the Midlands the master-stockinger was rarely regarded as a friend; and in Lancashire when people heard a story of distress they sometimes said, 'It 'ud melt th' heart of a whetstone, or what's harder a putter-eaut.'

Except in agriculture most of the workers were paid by the piece. In many industries it was usual for them to receive a round sum weekly or fortnightly to cover subsistence, and the balance of their earnings (if any) at the end of a period of six, eight, or twelve weeks. In the Midlands and South Wales the miners were engaged, not only to hew and draw the coal, but also to deliver it to the customer: they were entitled to payment only when it had been sold, and a delay in transport or the closing of a market might mean that they were deprived of their earnings for many weeks or even months. Such an arrangement threw the risks of production on to the shoulders of those least able to bear them; and, in all industries in which the 'long pay' existed, the workers tended to spend freely, even lavishly, for a few days after the pay, and to live for the rest of the time at a level of comfort far below that which a more rational distribution of resources would have afforded. It was not until after the industrial revolution, when the employers assumed fully the function of providing capital and bearing risks, that regularity of wage payment and, with it, regularity of expenditure were attained.

Many workers received their earnings, not from their employer or his agent, but from a superior workman. This was so in those areas of coal-mining in which the butty system prevailed; it was so in the east of Scotland where the woman 'fremd' bearer was bound to the hagger or collier and received her pittance from him, and to some extent in Northumberland and Durham where the pitmen employed and paid the 'foals' or 'colts', who were often their own children. In many of the metal trades, in pin-making, and in the varied crafts of London, production was carried on by outworkers who employed other journeymen; and even in the highly organized establishment of Ambrose Crowley the smiths, following the custom of the trade, paid their own hammermen. The London silk-weavers hired women to wind and children to fill the quills for their shuttles. Almost everywhere there was a degraded form of apprenticeship, of both boys and girls, which offered little or no training; and many children suffered from hunger, over-work, and ill-treatment. It was not in industries like iron-smelting, where large-scale capital and well-to-do employers ruled, but in the poorly developed domestic trades, that the conditions of labour were at their worst.

The more highly skilled workers in agriculture, and in the

coal, iron, pottery, and other trades, were hired for long periods, usually for the year. The bonds under which they served gave them some security of employment and, incidentally, were a safeguard against conscription into the Forces of the Crown—a body of poor repute which only the destitute would join of their own free will. But the price of security was the loss of freedom to move. The Scottish colliers and salt-workers were guaranteed subsistence, but they were bound, by custom and law, to work at the same place and the same job for life. And even in England, where such conditions of serf-dom had long been swept away, it was a question whether the lot of the skilled worker was more eligible than that of the labourer or semi-skilled weaver, who, if he was often without employment, might change his occupation, and (within the limits of the laws of Settlement) his place of work, at will.

There were many sources of industrial disharmony, especially in the domestic trades. Some employers used false weights in giving out yarn or iron, and demanded from the workers more cloth or nails than the material would run to. Others gave out faulty raw material or were irregular in their payments. In the more remote areas, where there were few retail shops, and where the supply of money was inadequate, truck was common. On the other hand, the spinners, weavers, knitters, nail-makers, and so on were often unpunctual in returning their work; textile workers mixed butter and grease with the fabric to increase the weight, and nail-makers substituted inferior iron for the rods they had received from the warehouse. Filch-ing of material was widespread. Acts of Parliament, with in-creasingly heavy penalties, were passed in 1703, 1740, 1749, and 1777, in an attempt to check it; and in the last of these years the employers were given the power to enter shops or out-houses for the purpose of search. At this time the first of a number of Worsted Committees was set up to deal with embezzlement and delays in the return of work. The inspectors appointed by them were licensed by the Justices and formed what was, in effect, an industrial police. In the wide areas in which they operated the workers were subject to a discipline little less complete than that of the factory-master, without the compensation in regularity of employment and hours that the factory was to offer.

The organization of production through a series of merchants and intermediaries necessitated a system of credit. But the obverse of credit is debt. The domestic workers were often debtors to their employers, not only for material, but also for sums of money borrowed to meet the emergencies of birth, sickness, death, or removal to a new home. The claims of the lender were met by deductions from future earnings, and sometimes children were set to work for the employer without wages, as a means of settlement. Often before one obligation was met a new one was incurred: wages books afford many instances of workers who were never free from debt. Goods were bought from pedlars on credit, ale scores were run up at the tavern, and when payment was demanded, a new call was made on the employer. In many towns special courts were set up for the recovery of small debts, as well as to deal with the theft of material. Indebtedness—especially indebtedness to an employer—must have weakened, not only the morals, but also the bargaining power of men and women who, at the best, were never in a position to argue effectively about wages.

There was a tendency for employers to spread work lightly over a large number of workers, partly to ensure that they would not be short of labour in times of pressure. The hosiers and stockingers had a special incentive to do this, for the more knitters they employed the greater their income from framerents. The skill needed for most domestic occupations was easily acquired, and the opportunity of employment for all members of the family acted as a magnet. Hence there was a tendency for more people to enter these trades than could be assured of regular work. Under-employment, rather than periodic unemployment, was the bane of the domestic worker.

It used to be commonly asserted that the existence of a supply of labour in excess of the demand was the result of 'the exhaustion of investment opportunities' which was said to be a feature of 'a late stage of capitalism'. But, in the period 1700–1760, before capitalism had come to maturity or opportunities of investment were fully open, large numbers of people had no regular means of employment. The beggars and vagrants, thieves and highwaymen, prostitutes and parasites of various kinds formed a much larger section of the population than today. But, these apart, there was a substantial body of men and women, on the fringe of the economic system, who eked out a living by honest means if they could—the squatters on the waste and the semi-employed cottagers and garret-dwellers of the towns. These formed a large part of that mass of the 'poor' whose untidy and imprudent manner of living was an affront to the reason and good sense of early economists like Dean Tucker. Some of them, indeed, were poor because of defects of character, but others because, at the prevailing level of investment, there was little or no work for them to do. It was not the least of the achievements of the industrial revolution that it drew into the economic system part of that legion of the lost, and that it turned many of the irregulars into efficient, if over-regimented, members of an industrial army.

To the question why the industrial revolution did not come earlier many answers can be given. In the first half of the eighteenth century there was much ingenuity and contrivance, but time was needed for this to reach fruition. Some of the early inventions failed because of incomplete thought, others because the right material was not to hand, because of lack of skill or adaptability on the part of the workers, or because of social resistance to change. Industry had to await the coming of capital in quantities large enough, and at a price low enough, to make possible the creation of the 'infrastructure'—of roads, bridges, harbours, docks, canals, waterworks and so on—which is a prerequisite of a large manufacturing community. It had to wait until the idea of progress—as an ideal and as a process at work in society—spread from the minds of the few to those of the many. But, such large considerations apart, in each of the major industries there was some obstacle—some bottle-neck, to use the current phrase—which had to be removed before expansion could go far. In agriculture it was the common rights and the lack of winter fodder; in mining the want of an efficient device to deal with flood water; in iron-making the shortage of suitable fuel; in the metal trades a consequent shortage of material; and in textiles an inadequate supply of yarn. Transport, trade, and credit alike suffered from the dead hand of monopolistic organization, and the arrested development of these services had adverse effects on industry in general. Thus it was that, though there was growth in every field of human endeavour, change was never so rapid as to endanger the stability of existing institutions. In the period 1700–1760 Britain experienced no revolution, either in the technique of production, the structure of industry, or the economic and social life of the people.

3
The Technical Innovations

'ABOUT 1760 a wave of gadgets swept over England.' So, not inaptly, a schoolboy began his answer to a question on the industrial revolution. It was not only gadgets, however, but innovations of various kinds—in agriculture, transport, manufacture, trade, and finance—that surged up with a suddenness for which it is difficult to find a parallel at any other time or place. The quickened pace of development is attested by the catalogue of new patents, the lengthening list of Acts of enclosure, the expanding figures of output and exports, and the course of prices, which, after remaining roughly steady for two generations, now began an ascent that was to continue for more than half a century. The story of a period the opening decade of which alone saw the innovations associated with the names of Brindley, Roebuck, Wedgwood, Hargreaves, Arkwright, and Watt can hardly be told in terms of an evolutionary process.

It has already been suggested that this period of time was propitious for invention and expansion. The fall in the rate of interest, coinciding as it did with an expansion of markets at home and abroad, provided the incentive. Pelham's conversion of the Debt from $3\frac{1}{2}$ to 3 per cent had been completed in 1757; and although the Seven Years War pressed down the price of Consols, and closed some doors to British trade, the return of peace in 1763 brought with it a rate for public borrowing which did not exceed $3\frac{3}{4}$ per cent, and an opening of new areas of enterprise and capital in the Far East and elsewhere. At the same time the barriers imposed by the shortages of food, fuel, iron, yarn, and transport were being thrown down at a speed which makes it difficult to determine where the priority lay. And just as an obstacle in the path of any one industry had led to congestion in that of others, so now its removal produced a widespread liberation. Innovation is a process which, once under way, tends to accelerate.

In agriculture enclosure went on apace. It spread from parishes where the occupiers were few to those where they were many; and, since there was hostility, it was necessary to proceed by Act of Parliament instead of by deed of mutual agreement. A petition signed by the owners of four-fifths of the land (but usually by a much smaller proportion of the number of owners) was sent to Westminster; and in due course a Bill was passed 'for dividing, allotting, and enclosing the open and common fields, meadows, pastures, and common and waste lands' of the particular parish. In the ten years beginning in 1740 there had been thirty-eight such Acts, and in the following ten years 156. But in the decade that opened in 1760 there were no fewer than 480, and much higher figures than this were to follow. The initiative usually came from the squire and the tithe-owner. A Parliament in which the landed interest was supreme paid little heed to protests. And, though the commissioners appointed under each separate Act seem to have been scrupulous in dealing with those who could establish a legal right to the land, they generally ignored the equitable claims of those whose only title was that they, and perhaps their forefathers, had tilled the soil, until now without challenge. The story of enclosures, indeed, fits well into the scheme of those who write economic history in terms of a class struggle, with the rich exerting political and economic power to impose their will on the poor. But the full story must also take account of a concerted effort to increase the productivity of the soil at a time when wars and bad harvests were threatening the existence of a growing urban society. There were many disreputable incidents associated with enclosure, but it is not enough to treat the whole movement as though it were just a smash-and-grab raid by a gang of aristocratic adventurers.

The open-field village was not wholly stagnant. In some

places new rotations, which included a crop of clover, had been introduced; but an Act of 1773, which sought to encourage such improvements by allowing the farmers to elect field-reeves, proved abortive. To close observers like Arthur Young the system appeared as a moribund survival of subsistence farming that must be swept away if England was to survive. In 1801—a year of war and also a year of famine—the General Enclosure Act simplified procedure and reduced costs, and from this time to 1815 the movement proceeded rapidly.

Not long ago it was generally believed that the enlosures were responsible for the decline of the yeoman freeholder, for a replacement of small estates by large, and for an extensive rural depopulation. It is true that there were fewer yeomen at the end of the eighteenth century than in earlier times; but recent statistical inquiries show that the freeholders had largely been bought out long before the period of Parliamentary enclosures. (After 1780, indeed, occupying ownership seems to have increased, for, as in 1914–20, many farmers made use of their wartime profits to purchase their holdings.) It is true that the larger farms tended to become bigger; but the number small enough to be worked by a single family also increased. It is true, once again, that where the enclosed land was turned to pasture less labour was required, and many cottars and squatters were bought out, or turned off. But, during the wars, when the urgent need was for more grain, the arable area, which required much labour, was expanding. Increasingly as time went on it was the waste that was the subject of enclosure, and the bringing into cultivation of land that had previously hardly been worked at all must have increased employment. Some agricultural workers, there is no doubt, migrated to nearby towns; but that they were attracted to manufacture, rather than repelled from agriculture, is indicated by the relatively high level of farm wages in the neighbourhood of the industrial centres. The fact that no single county of England registered a decline of population between 1801 and 1851 suggests that there was no widespread de-peopling of the countryside at this time.

The technical developments of the period were not, indeed,

of a labour-saving kind. Farming offers relatively little scope for specialization, and extensive use of machinery on the land came only with the twentieth century. In the 1780s new types of ploughs were introduced, and a Scottish millwright devised a more efficient threshing machine. The increased output of iron led to a substitution of metal for wood in the frame of the plough, as well as in parts of the harrow and the roller; and in 1803 a ploughshare of steel was put on the market. None of these innovations, however, was of consequence: it is in other directions that we must look for the major changes in agricultural technique.

In 1760, Joseph Elkington began to develop new methods of drainage in Warwickshire. About the same time Robert Bakewell (1725–94) of Dishley in Leicestershire, using empirical methods of inbreeding, was producing cattle which gave a bigger yield of beef, as well as horses of greater power, and sheep of larger size and weight. From the late seventies Coke of Holkham (1752–1842) was expending vast sums on the improvement of his estate, making use of marls and clover, introducing new grasses and artificial feeds, giving inducements to tenants to keep their land in good heart, and advertising widely the merits of Norfolk husbandry. Other aristocrats, and George III himself, took up with enthusiasm the cause of agricultural improvement. Knowledge of new methods was spread at tenants' dinners, shearing feasts, and the more frequent meetings of many local farmers' clubs. The Society of Arts offered prizes for new devices, and the institution of county and regional agricultural societies aided the process. In 1776 there appeared the first number of the *Farmers' Magazine,* and in 1806 that of the *Farmers' Journal.* Treatises on agricultural methods and publications like those in which Arthur Young described his rides through England, Ireland, France, Italy, and Spain, helped to break down the isolation and parochialism of rural life. And in 1793 Sir John Sinclair (1745–1835) set up, with some support from Government, a voluntary society known as the Board of Agriculture, the reports of which have much to say of the experiments that were being made by obscure farmers in many parts of the country. There is, however, a danger of assuming that the improvements made by enlightened landlords and progressive cultivators were typical. The Norfolk rotation, the improved methods of breeding, the Rotherham plough, the substitution of the horse for the ox, and of wheat for rye or oats, were innovations that spread slowly. It was only in the East and East Midland counties that progress was marked, and in many parts of the country farming was carried on very much as it had been centuries before.

Production for the market, together with improved transport, encouraged a growth of geographical specialization and of trade between one region and another. The eastern and southern areas gave primacy to grain, the Midlands to cattle and horses, and the Home Counties to dairy produce and vegetables. Cattle were brought from Scotland to East Anglia, and from Wales to Essex, to be fattened for the market. Lambs were sent from Wiltshire to Middlesex, and from Nottingham to Worcester, and ewes for breeding came back in exchange. There were many minor specialisms—Cheshire cheese, Norfolk turkeys, Aylesbury ducks, Kent hops, and Hampshire honey. But the technical advantages of mixed farming were so great that the concentration was rarely, if ever, absolute.

Custom came to play a smaller, and competition a larger part in the determination of rents and wages. There was a rise in the standard of life of the labourers, at least in the North, though the decline of rural crafts pressed hard on many family budgets. But the workers had less security than in the past: with the improvements in threshing of the 1820s, there was less occupation on farms in the winter months, and the agricultural labourer began to share with the townsman the experience of technological unemployment. To the townsman himself, the progress of farming brought little but gain. Wheat came to take the place of rye and barley as the staple foods in the Midlands, and of oatmeal in the North and Scotland. Potatoes were brought into general use, and meat was no longer a luxury. A better and more varied diet was not without effect on the health and expectation of life of the workers, nor was it least among the causes of expansion of industrial output.

Like agriculture, the mining of coal offered little scope for the application of machinery or sudden changes in technique. Here, as in all extractive industries, progress was by small increments. The introduction of ponies into the pits of the North, about the middle of the century, greatly reduced the cost of coal, for it meant that the barrowmen, who had formed the majority of the underground workers, could now be replaced by boys, whose wages were relatively low. The increased output of iron, itself based on coal, had important effects on mining practice. The use of cast-iron tubbing in the shaft made it possible to sink to greater depths; and the cast-iron rail, which John Curr intoduced into the pits about Sheffield in 1777, effected a further economy in underground transport. The wheeled corf which he devised to run on the rails could be brought up the shaft without being unloaded at the pit bottom, and this again meant a lowering of costs. Methods of ventilation were improved when, in the fifties, Carlisle Spedding of Whitehaven introduced the use of brattices to guide the air through the underground ways, and still more, in the nineties, when John Buddle brought into the Northumberland field his system of triple shafts and more elaborate methods of 'coursing'. The process of hewing the coal remained much as before, but the supporting pillars of coal were 'robbed' until they became slender columns; and towards the end of the century gunpowder came into use for blasting the rock. Illumination continued to present a major problem until, in 1813–15, Sir Humphry Davy, Dr. Clanny, and George Stephenson produced their several safety lamps, the first application of which brought, it is said, not greater security of life for the miner, but a larger output of coal—from seams that had previously been considered too dangerous to be worked at all.

In the iron industry the coke-fed blast furnaces had been growing steadily in size and number, and new areas of enterprise had been opened up. Stimulated by the demand for munitions, many new works, including those of John Wilkinson at Broseley and of John Roebuck at Carron, were set up during the war of 1756–63. In its magnitude and the variety of its products (which included the famous carronades) the Carron ironworks was a portent of a new type of undertaking; and the lighting of its first furnace, on Boxing Day, 1760, may serve to mark, for those who like to be precise in such matters, the beginning of the industrial revolution in Scotland.

Though charcoal had still to be used in converting the coke-smelted pig into bar iron, mineral fuel was increasingly employed in the early stages of this process; and the brothers Cranage, who were employees of the Coalbrookdale Company, came near to success in their attempt to use coke alone for the purpose in 1766. It was not, however, until 1783–4 that a final solution was reached, when Henry Cort (1740–1800), a Navy agent who had set up a forge near Fareham, took out his two patents for puddling and rolling. Cort's method was first to re-heat the pig iron with coke until it was in a pasty form, then to stir it with iron rods until much of the carbon and impurities had been burnt away, and finally to pass it between iron rollers which pressed out the dross that remained. His discovery was one of the outstanding events in the history of technology. It had the effect of freeing the forge-masters from their dependence on the woodlands, just as Darby's discovery had freed the furnace owners. It liberated Britain from the necessity of importing large amounts of charcoal-iron from the Baltic, at a time when political relations with Sweden and Russia were liable to rupture. It drew the forge branch of the industry from its scattered haunts to the coalfields, where the making of finished iron could be carried on in close proximity to the furnaces. And it led to the growth of great integrated establishments, in which all processes, from the mining of ore and coal to the slitting of rods, were controlled by a single group of proprietors. Within a relatively short space of time the industry came to be concentrated in four main areas, and new types of communities, with dense populations, grew up around the pit-hills and slagheaps of Staffordshire, South Yorkshire, the Clyde, and South Wales. The output of iron increased vastly; metal came to take the place of timber and stone in works of construction; the hardware industries expanded the range of their products; and there was hardly an activity—from agriculture to ship-building, from engineering to weaving—that did not experience the animating effects of cheap iron.

A generation or so later came the discovery by David Mushet of the black-band ironstone in Scotland, and close on the heels of this the introduction by J. B. Neilson of the hot-blast, which resulted in a further increase in the output of the furnace. The dates of these inventions fall within the bounds of our period, but it was not until the thirties and forties that their full effects were felt.

Cort's invention of puddling and rolling, like many other technical inventions of the time, could not have been effective without the aid of a new form of power. Until the sixties of the eighteenth century Newcomen's engine remained a contrivance for the useful but limited purpose of pumping water. It is true that the water, raised to a height, could be used to drive a wheel and so to work machines of various kinds; but the expenditure of energy involved in the process was great—so great that a Scot, at any rate, could not bear to see it. At the University of Glasgow, Joseph Black (1728–99) was delivering lectures on the phenomenon (which he had discovered) of latent heat, and John Anderson was making use, in his class on Natural Philosophy, of a model of the engine. Not himself a member of the University, but a mathematical instrument-maker whose shop was within the precincts, James Watt (1736–1819) was called upon to repair the model. He saw that the chief defect of the atmospheric engine arose from the alternate injection and condensation of steam: in order to prevent the steam from condensing before the piston had completed its upward stroke, it was necessary to keep the cylinder warm; but, equally, in order to condense the steam for the return stroke, it was necessary for it to be cold. The sudden changes in the temperature of the cylinder wall meant that a great amount of potential energy ran to waste.

Watt had had many conversations with Black, Anderson, John Robison, and other members of the University about these things, and had pondered deeply on them for many months. Then, by a sudden flash of inspiration which came, in 1765, in the course of a Sunday afternoon stroll across the Green, he hit on the solution of introducing a separate condenser which could be kept permanently cool while the cylinder could be kept permanently hot. Within a few weeks a model was made, but many years were to pass before the technical difficulties of translating this into a full-scale engine were overcome. Watt's experiments were financed by John Roebuck, who held a share in the patent which was taken out in 1769. But the Carron ironworks could not supply the skilled artisans whose help was essential, and most of Watt's own energies had to be given to earning a living by work as a surveyor and civil engineer. In 1774, however, Roebuck, whose affairs had become embarrassed, transferred his share in the patent to Matthew Boulton (1728–1809), and James Watt left Scotland for Birmingham. Here he had the support of a man, already well established in business, endowed with a sanguine temperament, and driven by an ambition which extended far beyond that of merely making money.

At Boulton's Soho works there were the craftsmen Watt needed to make the valves and other delicate parts of the engine. Not far away was the Coalbrookdale ironworks, with its long experience of producing castings for the atmospheric engine, and near at hand, at Bradley, was the great ironmaster, John Wilkinson (1728–1808), whose patent, of 1774, for boring cannon could be adapted to boring cylinders with an accuracy that had not hitherto been attained. Watt was fortunate in his associates. The researches of Black, who laid down the first principles, the capital and enterprise of Boulton, the ingenuity of Wilkinson, the technical skill of Murdoch, Southern, and a host of obscure artificers, were all necessary to the making of the steam engine. It was Watt's merit, not only that he was among the first to apply to industry the methods of systematic experiment used in pure science, but that he was able to synthesize the ideas of others and bring together the varied skills required for the creation of a complex mechanism.

In 1775 Parliament extended Watt's patent for a further quarter of a century to 1800. During the first six years of this period the engine remained a single-acting device for producing a reciprocating stroke. It had an efficiency four times that of the atmospheric engine, and was used extensively for pumping water at reservoirs, brine works, breweries, and distilleries, and in the metal mines of Cornwall. In the coal industry, however, it played a relatively small part. For Watt based his premiums on the difference between the fuel consumption of the Newcomen engine and that of his own; and since, at the collieries, economy of small coal was of no consequence, there was little incentive to substitute new engines for old. In the iron industry, on the other hand, the contrivance was used to raise water to turn the great wheels which operated the bellows, forge hammers, and rolling mills; and, even at this first stage of development, it had important effects on output.

If Watt had done no more than this he would have established a claim to a place in the front rank of British inventors. But he could not rest satisfied with having made improvements, however great, in what was little more than a steam pump. His mind had long been busy with the idea of converting the to-and-fro action into a rotary movement, capable of turning machinery, and this was made possible by a number of devices, including the sun-and-planet, a patent for which was taken out in 1781. In the following year came the double-acting, rotative engine, in which the expansive force of steam was applied to both sides of the piston; in 1784 the parallel motion; and in 1788 the beautiful device of the governor, which gave the greater regularity and smoothness of working essential in a prime mover for the more delicate and intricate of industrial processes.

The introduction of the rotative engine was a momentous event. Coinciding in time as it did with that of Cort's puddling and rolling of iron, and following closely on the inventions of Arkwright and Crompton, it completely transformed the conditions of life of hundreds of thousands of men and women. After 1783, when the first of the new engines was erected—to work a hammer for John Wilkinson at Bradley—it became clear that a technological revolution was afoot in Britain. Before their patents expired in 1800, Boulton and Watt had built and put into operation about 500 engines, of both types, at home and (in a few instances) abroad. The new form of power, and, no less, the new transmitting mechanisms by which this was made to do work previously done by hand and muscle, were the pivot on which industry swung into the modern age.

It was in the manufacture of textiles that the transformation was most rapid. Already, important changes had come about in spinning, and the problem of the shortage of yarn, which had for so long held back the development of weaving, had been solved. Some time between 1764 and 1767, James Hargreaves, a weaver-carpenter of Blackburn, had devised a simple hand machine, called the jenny, by means of which a woman could spin, at first six or seven, but later as many as eighty, threads at once. Unfortunately for him, he made and sold a number of jennies before he took out a patent in 1770, and for this reason it was later held in the courts that his claim was invalid. The jenny was adopted with enthusiasm, first in Nottingham, and afterwards in Lancashire; and by 1788 there were, it is estimated, about 20,000 of the machines at work in England. The jenny was small enough to be housed in a cottage; it was cheap to construct; and no great strength was needed to operate it. Hence it fitted well into the existing framework of domestic industry; and, since the spinner was now able to keep pace with the weaver, the effect was to strengthen, rather than weaken, the family economy. The jenny-spun yarn, however, was soft, and suitable therefore only for weft; the warp had still to be spun on the hand-wheel, until, following close on the invention of Hargreaves, came that connected with the name of Arkwright.

Richard Arkwright (1732–92) was a barber and wig-maker of Preston. Not himself, it would seem, of any great inventive ability, he had the force of character and robust sense that are traditionally associated with his native county—with little, it may be added, of the kindliness and humour that are, in fact, the dominant traits of Lancashire people. Helped by a Warrington clock-maker, John Kay (who had assisted Thomas Highs of Leigh in experiments in spinning), he produced, in 1768, the 'frame', a patent for which was granted to him in the following year. In appearance the frame was similar to the contrivance of Lewis Paul—it made use of rollers to draw out the rovings before these passed to the spindle—though whether or not Arkwright, Kay, or Highs had actually seen a machine of Paul's construction must remain in doubt. The product was a strong, if somewhat coarse, twist, suitable for warps, and less expensive than the linen that had generally been used for the purpose. It was on the basis of cheap calicoes, made entirely of cotton, that the first stage of the industrial revolution in textiles was built.

Like Hargreaves, Arkwright soon left Lancashire for Nottingham where the demand of the hosiers offered an immediate market for his yarn. Unlike the jenny, the frame required, for its working, power greater than that of human muscles, and hence from the beginning the process was carried on in mills or factories. After experiments in small establishments in which the power was provided by horses, Arkwright sought the support of the well-to-do hosiers, Samuel Need of Nottingham and Jedediah Strutt of Derby. In 1771 he set up a large water-driven factory at Cromford—modelled, it is said, on Lombe's silk works at Derby—where within a very short time he was giving employment to about 600 workers, most of them children. It soon became apparent that the older methods of carding were no longer able to supply material in quantities sufficient to meet the needs of the spinners; and in 1775, drawing together the ideas of others, and adding to these the crank and comb, Arkwright obtained a patent for carding by cylinders. This, like spinning by rollers, required extra-human power, and henceforth it was usual for the two processes to be carried on, side by side, in the factory. New mills were set up at Belper and Milford in Derbyshire, and in 1777 the first of the water-driven factories in Lancashire was erected near Chorley. After 1781 when the Manchester cotton-spinners (determined opponents of all forms of monopoly as they were) succeeded in getting the carding patent revoked, hundreds of workmen were busy running up new factories in the countryside, not only of Lancashire but also of Cheshire, Derbyshire, Nottinghamshire, Yorkshire, and North Wales.

About the middle of the eighties the situation was again changed by yet another innovation in spinning. After seven years of experiment in his 'conjuring room' at Hall-i'-th'-Wood, a Bolton weaver, Samuel Crompton (1753–1827), succeeded in producing a yarn, at once strong, fine and even, suitable for both warp and weft, and adapted to the making of all kinds of textiles, but especially to that of the fine muslins which had hitherto been imported as a luxury from the East. The machine had features of both the jenny and the water-frame and, because of its supposed cross-bred origin, came to be known as the 'mule'. Probably because the wide terms of Arkwright's specification barred the way, no patent was taken out. And when, in 1785, both of Arkwright's patents were finally cancelled, the field for enterprise was open to all. In the same year Watt's steam engine was first applied to spinning by rollers, and, after 1790, when steam power was used to drive the mules, it became possible to put up large factories in towns. This did not mean, however, that the country factories declined: on the contrary, their numbers increased steadily until about the end of the first decade of the new century—partly because the machines driven by water were subject to less vibration, and were therefore better for spinning fine counts, than those driven by steam. But the growth of the urban factories was rapid: whereas in 1782 there had been only two cotton mills in and about Manchester, in 1802 the number had reached fifty-two; and by 1811 four-fifths of the cotton goods produced in Lancashire were made of mule yarn, most of it spun in the towns.

In the late eighties and nineties the demand for the new muslins was so great that the weavers of these (though not the weavers of coarser cloths) experienced high prosperity. There was, indeed, a boom, and large numbers of men and women were drawn into the weaving branch of the industry. This was the period which saw a rapid conversion of barns and brewhouses into weaving sheds, and the throwing up of 'loom houses', attached to cottages, all over the countryside. But the 'golden age of the weavers' was not destined to last. Already in 1784, a clergyman-poet, Edmund Cartwright, foreseeing the developments that would follow the end of Arkwright's patents, had devised a power-loom which could be operated by horses, water-wheels, or steam engines. Unlike the devices for spinning, the power-loom made relatively slow progress: many improvements had to be brought about in the loom before it could be an effective instrument of factory production. New contrivances for dressing the warp and taking up the cloth on the beam were introduced by William Radcliffe and Thomas Johnson in 1803 and 1804; and further developments were made in the following decade by Horrocks of Stockport and Roberts of Manchester. But even in 1813 it was estimated that there were not more than 2,400 power-looms in the country, as against nearly a hundred times that number of looms operated by hand. After the end of the French war the pace of development quickened: by 1820 there were about 14,000 and by 1833 about 100,000 power-looms in Britain. The attempt of the hand-loom weavers to compete with steam and the superior organization of the factory forms the subject of one of the most depressing chapters in the economic history of the period.

In many cases weaving was carried on by independent employers who specialized in this branch of the industry; but after 1820 a tendency developed for spinners to attach weaving sheds to their mills. As in the manufacture of iron, so in that of cotton, industrial change was associated with the rise of large concerns and integration of processes.

Most of the innovations in spinning and weaving cotton were applicable to the manufacture of other textile fabrics. But technological progress was, in fact, far less rapid in the woollen and worsted than in the cotton industry: even in the middle of the nineteenth century not more than half the Yorkshire textile workers, and still less of those of the West Country, had been brought into factories. The reason for this does not lie (as some have supposed) in innate conservatism: Yorkshiremen were then, as now, as alert and energetic as Lancastrians. It lay partly in the nature of the raw material; partly in the regulations which well-intentioned, but ill-informed, governments had made for the conduct of the industry; and partly in the fact that the demand for woollen cloths, at home and abroad, was less elastic than that for calicoes and muslins. Here and there large factories were set up by enterprising merchants like Benjamin Gott. But the typical business was a relatively small concern, owned by several men, who were associated as equals in what was, in effect, a joint-stock company. A few not inconsiderable fortunes were made in the West Riding, but there was no Arkwright or Peel, no woollen king to vie with the cotton kings to the west of the Pennines.

The later processes in the manufacture of cotton underwent changes hardly less great than those in carding, spinning, and weaving. In the early years of the eighteenth century the printing of calicoes had been done by craftsmen who, making use of wooden blocks, impressed the pattern on the cloth by hand. The first innovation was the substitution of plates of copper; but the greatest step forward was made in 1783, when a Scot, Thomas Bell, replaced these by large revolving cylinders worked by power. His invention was at once adopted by the Peels and others in Lancashire, and the era of large-scale production in calico printing thus coincided almost precisely with that in carding and spinning. The other finishing processes of bleaching and dyeing were less susceptible of machine methods. But in these also a long series of innovations culminated, about the same time, in a revolution of technique and the growth of large-scale undertakings. The story is closely bound up with that of the discovery of new reagents and tinctures, largely by Scottish and French scientists, and with the rise of industrial chemistry in England.

The traditional method of bleaching was to expose the fabric to the rays of the sun, or to boil it, first in a solution of ashes and then in sour milk. The publication, in 1756, by an Edinburgh professor, Francis Home, of his *Art of Bleaching* pointed to the replacement of the sour milk by sulphuric acid, a material which was already in limited use for cleaning tinplate and other products of the metal trades. In 1736, an apothecary, Joshua Ward, had set up at Twickenham works in which, making use of an apparatus of glass, he was able to produce vitriol on a small scale. But the cost was great, and the real beginnings of industrial sulphuric acid came ten years or so later when John Roebuck, himself a trained chemist, joined with Samuel Garbett to establish works, first at Birmingham and later at Prestonpans, in which the acid was produced in vessels of lead. In 1787 Berthollet's process of bleaching by chlorine was brought from France by James Watt, and used by Watt's father-in-law, M'Gregor, and others in Scotland. And in 1798 Charles Tennant of Glasgow discovered a method of passing chlorine gas over slaked lime, and so of producing a bleaching powder, easier to handle and transport, and less injurious to health, than the liquid acids.

The production of bleaching materials was only one side of the application of chemistry to industry. Parallel to, and connected with, the manufacture of acids was that of alkalis and salts. At Prestonpans Roebuck had made use of vitriol and common salt to produce soda, and in 1773 James Keir (who had studied chemistry under Black and had served with Wolfe at Quebec) joined with another ex-serviceman, Alexander Blair, to set up works at Tipton. Here they made soda for the soapmakers, white lead for the potters, and litharge for the glassworks which they had themselves established earlier at Stourbridge. Other manufacturers engaged in the production of potash, alum, and ammonia, a method of making the last of which had been discovered by Priestley a few years earlier. At a later stage saltwater, coal, and supplies of sulphuric acid attracted the rising chemical industry to the area about the Tyne, where, early in the nineteenth century, the introduction by the Cooksons of the Leblanc process led to a rapid concentration of population about South Shields and Gateshead. But the greatest development came in the early twenties, when, encouraged by the reduction of the duties on salt, James Muspratt and Josiah Gamble left Ireland to exploit the Leblanc process at Liverpool. It was out of their concerns that there were to arise, later, the thriving, if unlovely, communities of St. Helens and Widnes.

Meanwhile, progress was being made with the derivatives of coal. As early as 1756 the Scottish geologist, James Hutton, had succeeded in extracting salammoniac from soot. But it was yet another Scot, Alexander Cochrane, ninth Earl of Dundonald, who was responsible for the real exploitation of coal as a source of chemicals. Throughout the eighteenth century tar and pitch, essential for the protection of the timbers of vessels, were almost a monopoly of the Baltic Powers, which were thus in a position to exert diplomatic pressure on a nation increasingly dependent for its prosperity on shipping. Patriotism and self-interest, alike, led the Earl to experiment in extracting tar and varnish from the coals of his estate and, in 1782, to set up works for the purpose at Culross. Several circumstances favoured the enterprise. Joseph Black, Adam Smith, and a relative, J. L. Macadam, gave counsel; Parliament extended the patent to 1806; and the rapid expansion of coke-ovens, following on the inventions of Henry Cort, provided in their waste gases raw material in the form required. But a shortage of capital, the conservatism of the Admiralty, and the temperament of Dundonald himself, led to financial loss. It was left to Macadam and his successors to reap the rewards of an innovation the potentialities of which have been fully realized only in our own day.

In the industries so far considered the growth of production was associated with new forms of power, new machinery, or new knowledge derived from science. That these were not the only influences shaping the industrial revolution is evident from the development that took place in the manufacture of pottery. From the seventeenth century a growing shortage of tin and lead, and a growing taste for tea and coffee, had brought a gradual substitution of earthenware for metal in household utensils of various kinds. Porcelain from the East and Delft ware from Holland had appeared on the tables of the well-to-do, and cruder English pottery on those of the relatively poor. In the early part of the eighteenth century there were potteries at Lambeth, Chelsea, Bristol, Worcester, Liverpool, and other urban centres; but the scarcity of wood fuel was driving the industry to the coalfields, and especially to north Staffordshire, where clays of various kinds and lead for glazing were close at hand. As in other trades producing consumers' goods, the works were small. The typical employer was a man who owned one or two sheds, a vat for mixing the clay with water, a sun-pan for evaporation, a single potter's wheel, worked by hand or foot, and an oven for baking the ware. The pots were sold to itinerant cratemen, who carried them away in panniers on the backs of donkeys. Progress was largely a matter of developing new skills and of finding better clays, glazing materials, and means of decoration. White clays from Devon and Dorset, mixed with calcined flints, replaced the coarser and duller clays of Staffordshire; salt was brought from Cheshire for glazing (though by no means to the exclusion of lead); cobalt came to be used for tinting; and plaster of Paris was employed for making the blocks or moulds in which the pottery was pressed or cast. About the middle of the century the 'pyrometric bead' was devised to measure the temperature of the ovens, and a little later came the use of copper plates for impressing designs on the ware.

In several of these developments a prominent part was played by the family of the Wedgwoods, members of which had been engaged in the industry from the early years of the seventeenth century: it is with Josiah Wedgwood (1730–95) that the growth of the Potteries is most closely linked. In 1769 he set up near Hanley the famous Etruria works which became, like Coalbrookdale, Cromford, and Soho, a model for many other undertakings. Though not a trained scientist, Wedgwood was tireless in experiment: he devised a green glaze, introduced the cream-coloured pottery known as Queen's ware, and perfected the jasper (white figures in relief against a coloured background) which comes to mind whenever the name of Wedgwood is mentioned today. He had artistic sensibilities and employed men of the quality of Flaxman and Webber to design his 'ornamental' products; but he had also the plain sense to know that his profits must come from the manufacture on a large scale of what he called 'useful' wares. A friend of Boulton and Watt, he took a keen interest in the development of the steam-engine, and made use of the new power for grinding materials and turning the lathes. But most of the work at Etruria was done by hand: it was by intensifying the division of labour that Wedgwood brought about the reduction of cost which enabled his pottery to find markets in all parts of Britain, and also in Europe and America. He built a village for his work-people, spent much money on the improvement of roads, and was Treasurer to the Grand Junction Canal, the opening of which, in 1777, brought a new era of prosperity to the Potteries, and to Etruria in particular. Though not the inventor of any one outstanding device, Wedgwood was an innovator of the first rank. He had the acumen to obtain a majority of the shares in the Cornish Clay Company, and his organizing abilities were shown, not only in the stress he laid on the training of labour, but also in the care he took in the selection of his salesmen and managers, and the attention he paid to the avoidance of waste. Beginning in humble circumstances, he died worth more than half a million, and in the process of making it he 'converted a rude and inconsiderable manufactory into an elegant art and an important element in national commerce'.

Among the new industries to which the eighteenth century gave rise perhaps the most important was engineering. It has been said that the civil engineer, as we know him today, is the lineal descendant of the military sapper of the wars of the seventeenth century. But, however it may have been in other parts of Europe, in England it was not strategic, but commercial, necessities that led to improvements in the means of communications: the men who made the new roads, bridges, canals, and railways were civilians employed, not by the State, but by individuals, or companies of men, eager to develop the trade of the area from which they derived their personal incomes. Prominent among them were the large landed proprietors, and foremost of these Francis Egerton, the second Duke of Bridgewater, who, it is said, laid out more than a quarter of a million pounds on the development of his coal works and canals.

It was in 1759 that the Duke, tired of London society and disappointed in love, took up a project that his father had formed to construct a canal from his coal mines at Worsley to the growing town of Manchester, a few miles away. This was a work of considerable difficulty, since it involved, on the one hand, carrying the navigation into the underground workings, and, on the other, erecting an aqueduct over the Irwell at Barton. But the skill of James Brindley (1716–72), an unlettered mill-wright who had entered the Duke's service, overcame all obstacles; and by the summer of 1761 coal was being delivered to Manchester at a cost of carriage half that at which it had previously been brought by road. When the Seven Years War ended in 1763, and the rate of interest fell, the Duke embarked on the more ambitious enterprise of extending his canal to Runcorn at the mouth of the Mersey, and so of providing an efficient line of communication between the textile region of south-east Lancashire and Liverpool. Before the new waterway was opened in 1767, plans were already on foot for a canal which, passing through the salt-mining area of Cheshire and the pottery area of Staffordshire, would connect the Mersey with the Trent, and so with the Humber. This Grand Trunk, as it was called, was an undertaking the execution of which required far more capital than could be raised privately. The Duke, his brother-in-law, Earl Gower, Lord Anson, the Marquis of Stafford, Josiah Wedgwood, Richard Bentley, and others joined hands to secure the necessary Act and provide the resources. And Brindley again supplied the skill and organizing ability for an enterprise which brought under unified direction a larger body of men than had ever previously been employed in any single operation short of a military campaign. Many difficulties, physical and financial, were encountered: it was not until 1777, years after Brindley, worn out by his efforts, had gone to his grave, that the Grand Trunk was completed.

Meanwhile, the Wolverhampton Canal, begun in 1768, had linked the metal-working Midlands with the Severn: it had a junction with the Grand Trunk, and the two navigations together thus provided continuous transport by water between Bristol, Liverpool, and Hull. The next objective of the projectors was London. In 1767 and 1768 Acts had been obtained for two canals, the Coventry and the Oxford, which were to give access to the Thames. But the outbreak of the American War brought a sharp rise in the rate of interest that made it difficult to raise capital, and it was not until 1790 that this major aim was achieved. In the meantime several other canals had been cut in the region about Birmingham and in the North. But it was in the period of cheap capital of the early nineties that activity in construction reached its peak. The canal mania of 1790–1794 undoubtedly led to some waste of national resources in ill-advised projects, but, taken as a whole, the investment in waterways brought, not only substantial dividends to shareholders, but an increase in the real income of the public in general.

The canal era was a short one—it coincided with the period 1760–1830—but it saw momentous changes in economic life. The cost of bulky or heavy commodities such as coal, iron, timber, stone, salt, and clay was greatly reduced; agricultural regions that had been remote from the market were brought within the widening circle of exchange; the fear of local famine, of both food and fuel, was removed; and the closer contact with others that the new means of communication afforded had a civilizing influence on the populations of the Potteries and other inland areas. There was a re-distribution of activities: old river ports such as Bewdley and Bawtry declined, and new communities grew up at nodal points like Stourport. The competitive position of the more distant centres of production was improved, and rents in those nearer to the markets fell, or failed to rise as they must otherwise have done. The incomes paid out to those who dug the new canals, when spent, resulted in the raising of the level of employment generally. The offer of transferable shares, with prospects of high profit, accustomed men to invest their resources outside the restricted field of the Funds and the chartered trading companies, and so played a part in the rise of an impersonal market for capital. Perhaps the most important result, however, of the movement initiated by Bridgewater and Brindley was that it trained up a new race of engineers, equipped to meet the calls which the age of railways was to make on their skill, endurance, and capacity for disciplined effort.

Parallel changes were made in the road system of Britain. In the first half of the century Acts had been passed to regulate such things as the weight of the load to be carried, the number of horses to a wagon, and the breadth of the rim of the wheels: the policy was one of making the traffic conform to the roads. After 1750, however, attempts were made to adapt the roads to the traffic. The number of turnpikes increased vastly, especially in the early fifties, and again in the early nineties, when rates of interest were low; and in the growing industrial regions of the North, in particular, several self-taught engineers did much to increase the carrying capacity of the highways. Among the pioneers was John Metcalf (1717–1810), who, in spite of blindness, constructed many new roads in Lancashire and Yorkshire, laying bunches of heather as a foundation where the sub-soil was soft, forming convex surfaces, and digging ditches to carry off the water which was the chief enemy of the road-maker, as of the miner. At a later stage came Thomas Telford (1757–1834), surveyor of the London-Holyhead road, architect of the beautiful Menai Bridge, and first President of the Society of Civil Engineers; and John Loudon Macadam (1756–1836), surveyor-general to the London turnpikes and the first great transport administrator. The methods of the two men were different: the first laid stress on solid foundations, the second on the use for the surface of broken stone or flint pressed so as to form a kind of arch. But, between them, they revolutionized travel. Wagons superseded pack-horses over much of the country; the number of public and private vehicles increased beyond measure; and, in the two decades that followed Waterloo, England passed into the era of flying coaches, busy wayside inns, and a preoccupation with the style and performance of horses that has not yet entirely disappeared. If the changes in the roads were of less moment to industry than those in the waterways, their effects on internal trade were significant; the commercial traveller came to take the place of the 'rider-out'; the Royal Mail became a more efficient channel of correspondence; and the processes of placing orders and remitting money were made more simple and speedy.

From early times it had been the practice at the larger collieries to lay down baulks of wood to facilitate the movement of the wagons that bore the coal to the rivers or the ports. In the early eighteenth century plates of cast iron were sometimes fixed to these at curves in the road or other points of exceptional friction. At a later stage, in 1767, Richard Reynolds constructed, from Coalbrookdale to the Severn, a track of cast-iron rails, which were furnished with flanges to hold the wheels to the line; and in 1789, following the advice of the famous engineer, John Smeaton, the flange was transferred from the rail to the wheel. So far, the rails had been used almost exclusively about coal mines and iron works. But in 1801 the Surrey Iron Railway was constructed from Wandsworth to Croydon, to carry goods for the public in general. During the following twenty years about a score of companies were authorized to run tramways, most of which, however, acted as feeders to the canals, rather than as alternative means of transport.

On all the early railroads traction was by horses. But from the 1760s many ingenious minds, in France as well as Britain, turned to the possibility of harnessing for carriage the newly discovered power of steam. In 1784 both William Symington and William Murdoch made model locomotives. But Watt, who was the arbiter on all matters relating to steam, looked on these as mere toys, and, largely because of his obstructive attitude, the idea of steam locomotion was put aside. After the expiration of Watt's patent the Cornish engineer, Richard Trevithick (1771–1833), devised a high-pressure engine; and, in 1803, a steam carriage of his construction made several journeys through the streets of London. Public highways, however, proved to be unsuited to locomotive traffic, and Trevithick's bold experiment bore no immediate fruit. The possibility of running the engine on specially constructed roads was delayed by the curious belief that a smooth wheel would not 'bite' on a smooth rail; it was not until 1812 that a colliery engineer, William Hedley, demonstrated the practicability of a union of the two devices. Shortly afterwards, another colliery enginewright, George Stephenson (1781–1848), raised the efficiency of the locomotive by increasing the draught to the fire-box;

and when, in 1821, Edward Pease and his fellow Quakers obtained powers to construct a railway from Stockton to Darlington, Stephenson was engaged as engineer, and his locomotive (together with horses and cables wound by stationary engines) was used for traction. It was not, however, until 1829, when Stephenson's Rocket won the competition at Rainhill on the newly constructed Liverpool and Manchester Railway, that the potentialities of steam transport were fully realized. The locomotive railway was the culminating triumph of the technical revolution: its effects on the economic life of Britain and, indeed, of the world have been profound. But the unfolding of these—and of the parallel consequences of steam navigation—belongs to a period beyond the limits of this book.

The production of engines was only one branch of that manufacture of machines which we call engineering. The modern fitter, turner, or pattern-maker can trace his pedigree back, beyond Stephenson, Watt, and Newcomen, to the millwright who was concerned with the creation and repair of water-wheels and the grinding apparatus which they worked. He can find ancestors, moreover, in the colliery viewers, clock-makers, instrument-makers, ironfounders, and cotton spinners, who, during the industrial revolution, turned from using to making the appliances of their trades. An important step in the building up of a specialized industry was taken in 1795, when Boulton and Watt ceased to be mere consultants (supplying plans, supervising the construction of engines, and drawing royalties) and established the Soho Foundry at Birmingham. About the same time, or a little later, a number of engineering workshops were set up in London by men like Joseph Bramah, Henry Maudslay, and Joseph Clement. And in the textile centres of Lancashire and Yorkshire, where previously the master-spinners had made their own machines, there sprang up works like those of Dobson and Barlow, Asa Lees, and Richard Roberts. Such establishments represented the external economies which are, at once, cause and effect of large-scale industry. The ingenious devices that flowed from them are too numerous to catalogue here: it must suffice to say that the more precise methods of planing, drilling, cutting, and turning they developed played a significant part in the later phase of the technical revolution in Britain.

So far the process of invention has been traced first in one industry and then in another. The arrangement has the merit of making clear what was involved in each successive step, but it fails to bring out the way in which discoveries in different fields of activity were linked together. Sometimes it was a simple case of imitation, as when the principle of attenuating material by passing it through rollers was transferred from the iron to the textile industry, or when Wilkinson's method of boring cannon was turned to the making of steam-engine cylinders. Sometimes an advance in one sphere was a condition of progress in another, as when the development of coke ovens made possible the extraction of tar. Often two or more industries went hand in hand, each contributing to the forward movement of the other. Without the discovery of smelting with coke, which made it possible to supply larger and more intricate castings, Newcomen could not have perfected his engine; and without Newcomen's engine Darby could hardly have obtained the blast that was necessary to produce iron on the scale required. Both the atmospheric and the steam engine helped to increase the output of coal and metals, and the larger supply of these (and especially of copper and brass) reacted on the development of engineering. 'Invention is the mother of necessity': an improvement in one process frequently put pressure on those concerned with an earlier, parallel, or later process in the same industry. The invasion by the founders of the territory of the forge-masters made these look to new ways of reducing the cost of wrought-iron; the introduction of the fly shuttle made it imperative for the spinners to seek out better methods of producing yarn; and the later improvements in spinning and weaving brought a new urgency to the search for quicker methods of bleaching and finishing. In all these ways innovation bred innovation.

The establishments at which each of the chief discoveries was first applied—Coalbrookdale, Cromford, Carron, Etruria, and Soho—became centres from which ideas and enterprise radiated to other parts of the land. The Darbys gave a training to men like Joseph and William Reynolds and the Cranage brothers; and from the Carron Ironworks proceeded those of the Clyde, Calder, Crammond, and Muirkirk companies. Arkwright's technique, and his methods of organizing labour, were copied by literally hundreds of master cotton-spinners in England, Scotland, and Wales. Boulton and Watt gave instruction to a generation of engineers which included Murdoch, Bull, Cameron, Southern, Ewart, and Brunton. And from a later school of engineering, Henry Maudslay's works in London, came Nasmyth, Clement, Roberts, Whitworth, and many more of their kind.

The development of invention is reflected in the tables of the Commissioners of Patents. Before the 1760s the number of patents granted in any single year rarely exceeded a dozen, but in 1766 it rose abruptly to 31, and in 1769 to 36. For some years the average remained below this figure, but in 1783 there was a sudden jump to 64. Thereafter the number fell, until in 1792 another bound brought it to 85. During the next eight years it fluctuated about a mean of 67, but from 1798 an upward movement brought it to a peak of 107 in 1802. Other pinnacles appeared in 1813 and 1818, but these were not outstanding. In 1824, however, the number of patents shot up suddenly once more—to 180—and in the following year of boom it attained the unprecedented height of 250. Those who take the perverse view that war is a spring of technological progress may be reminded that each of the major peaks—1766, 1769, 1783, 1792, 1802, and 1824–5—came in a time of peace. And those who believe that the wind bloweth where it listeth may well ponder the fact that at each of these dates the rate of interest was below the prevailing level, and that at each of them expectations of profit were running high.

When the inventions are set in chronological order it is possible to detect one or two distinct phases. In the early years of the eighteenth century effort was directed mainly to the harnessing of forces external to man. At Coalbrookdale energy stored up in coal was the essential element in smelting, atmospheric pressure the power that worked the pumps, and gravitation the force by which the water, thus brought to a head, turned the great wheel that operated the bellows. From the thirties and forties, when capital was relatively abundant, and industrial workers still relatively scarce, attention was centred on labour-saving mechanisms, such as those of Kay and Paul in the textile industries; and the search continued until, in the sixties and seventies, it culminated in the appliances of Hargreaves, Arkwright, and Crompton. But by this time the nature of the economic problem was changing: population was beginning to press on resources,. The quickening of the pace of enclosure and the breaking in of the waste were the outcome of a growing demand for food; Watt's first engine and the Duke's canals were the answer to a problem set by a shortage of coal; Cort's introduction of puddling and rolling was a measure to counter the continued famine of charcoal; and the researches of Dundonald and others may be thought of as the response of ingenuity to an insufficient supply of other raw materials. Towards the end of the century and later, when rates of interest were moving up, some (though by no means all) of the inventors turned their minds to capital-saving ends. The newer types of engine of Bull and Trevithick, and the newer ways of transmitting power, dispensed with much costly equipment; the newer methods of bleaching were economical of time; and the improved means of transport, with their greater speeds, released capital that had hitherto been locked up in goods on their way from producer to manufacturer, or manufacturer to consumer. It would be dangerous, however, to press these generalizations far. There was often a lag of years between an invention and its application, and it was this last, rather than the discovery itself, that was influenced by such things as a growing shortage of materials or a change in the supply of labour or capital. But, timing apart, it is important in each case to be clear whether the effect was to substitute natural resources or capital for labour, labour for capital, or one kind of labour for another. For on this depended the distribution, not merely among factors of production, but also among the different social classes, of the increased wealth to which the inventions gave rise.

It should be borne in mind that the field in which innovation took place was only a part of the national economy: it covered little more than the industries concerned with appliances and those intermediate products like yarn and cloth, that are included in the category of capital goods. The varied trades that provided things for the ultimate consumer were (apart from the pottery trade) hardly affected immediately. There were, in 1830, considerable areas of rural Britain, and many country towns, in which life went on in much the same way as a hundred years or more before. And even in the regions about London, Manchester and Birmingham there were men and women who toiled laboriously, without the aids that science and ingenuity had brought to their fellows in the factory, the foundry, and the mine.

4
Capital and Labour

I

THE industrial revolution was an affair of economics as well as of technology: it consisted of changes in the volume and distribution of resources, no less than in the methods by which these resources were directed to specific ends. The two movements were, indeed, closely connected. Without the inventions industry might have continued its slow-footed progress—firms becoming larger, trade more widespread, division of labour more minute, and transport and finance more specialized and efficient—but there would have been no industrial revolution. On the other hand, without the new resources the inventions could hardly have been made, and could never have been applied on any but a limited scale. It was the growth of savings, and of a readiness to put these at the disposal of industry, that made it possible for Britain to reap the harvest of her ingenuity.

There has been much discussion as to the origin of the capital that went into the expanding industries. Some say that it came from the land; others that it arose out of overseas trade; and yet others claim to have charted a current flowing from the secondary to the primary industries within the country. But for each piece of evidence it is possible to present counter-evidence. Many owners or occupiers of land, like Robert Peel, took to manufacture; but many successful manufacturers, like Arkwright, bought estates and finished as improving landlords. Many merchants, such as Anthony Bacon, reinvested their profits in mines or manufacture, but many industrialists, such as

Sampson and Nehemiah Lloyd and Peter Stubs, began to market the things they produced and also to sell for others. Many craftsmen who worked in metal, like Abraham Darby, set up furnaces and forges and sank mines; but many miners and ironmasters pushed forward into the hardware and tool-making trades. If landowners like the Duke of Bridgewater put capital into turnpikes and canals, so also did manufacturers like Wedgwood. The currents flowed in all directions as wealth increased here, and opportunities there: it was from no single zone of thrift and enterprise that the trade winds blew.

In the early years of the period many of the industrial units were small family concerns or partnerships of two or three friends. In most industries the fixed capital required was not more than a domestic manufacturer, or even a workman, could supply from his earnings. If a profit were made it was possible to use it to extend the plant: 'ploughing back' is not, as some have supposed, a transatlantic discovery of the twentieth century. The early stages of accumulation can be illustrated by quotations from the diary of Samuel Walker of Rotherham:

1741. In or about October or November of the same year, Saml. and Aaron Walker built an Air Furnace in the old nailer's smithy, on the backside of Saml. Walker's cottage at Grenoside, making some small additions thereto, and another little hutt or two, slating with sods etc., with a small Garth walled in: and after rebuilding the chimney or stacks once, and the furnace once or more, began to proceed a little, Saml. Walker teaching the school at Grenoside, and Aaron Walker making nails and mowing and shearing, etc., part of his time.

1743. Aaron Walker now began to be pretty much imploy'd, and had 4 shillings a week to live upon. . . .

1745. This year Saml. Walker, finding business increase, was obliged to give up his school, and built himself a house at the end of the old cottage, then thought he was fixed for life; then we allowed ourselves ten shillings a week each for wages to maintain our families.

At this time the value of the concern was put at £400. But in the following year £100 was added by Jonathan Walker (a brother of Samuel and Aaron), £50 by John Crawshaw (who had previously been employed 'as much as we could, at 12 pence per day'), and £50 by Samuel himself. Thus equipped, the partners set up at Masborough first a casting house and then, in 1748, a steel furnace. The story that Samuel Walker rose to fortune by stealing from Huntsman the secret of crucible steel has no foundation: it was not by such methods, but by unremitting labour, thrift, and integrity that success was achieved. Year after year some addition, great or small, was made to the plant. In 1754 a warehouse was built, and a keel—characteristically called *The Industry*—was put on the river. Four years later the partners dug 'a navigable cut' and 'improved the road from Holmes to Masbro' and lanes towards Tinsley—Gloria Deo'; and in 1764 they added to their establishment 'a large shop for frying pan makers'. It was not, apparently, until 1757, when the stock had reached £7,500, that the Walkers allowed themselves a dividend—of £140; and throughout, the proportion of the profit that was distributed remained small. Thus it came about that by 1774 the capital had reached £62,500. Profits on the manufacture of guns during the American War, ploughed back as they were, had, by 1782, raised the figure to £128,000. In this year Samuel Walker died, but the policy laid down by him was continued by his heirs, and in 1812 the assets of Samuel Walker & Co. were estimated at £299,015, and those of a sister concern, Walker and Booth, at a further £55,556.

Whatever may be said against the early employers, the charge of self-indulgence can hardly be laid at their door. The records of firm after firm tell the same story as that of the Walkers: the proprietors agreed to pay themselves small salaries, restrict their household expenses, and put their profits to reserves. It was in this way that Wedgwood, Gott, Crawshay, Newton Chambers & Co., and scores of others built up their great concerns. 'Industrial capital has been its own chief progenitor.'

From time to time, however, a business might require more funds than the most rigid economy could wring from internal sources. It was sometimes possible to obtain additional capital by taking in a new partner, active or sleeping. But the Bubble

Act of 1720 restricted an ordinary partnership to six members, each of whom was liable 'to his last shilling and acre' for the debts of the concern, and it was not easy to induce men of substance to assume such risks. Hence it was more usual to raise resources by mortgaging the factory buildings to some neighbouring landowner, solicitor, clergyman, or widow. As the return on investment in the public Funds fell, a mortgage at 5 per cent became an attractive security; and throughout the industrial revolution—until, indeed, the coming of limited liability in the fifties and sixties of the nineteenth century—it remained an important instrument of industrial finance. Sometimes loans could be obtained, either in this way or on personal security, from friends or men engaged in the same field of activity: Abraham Darby provided capital for a number of fellow Quakers in the iron industry; Roebuck borrowed from Boulton, Arkwright from Strutt, and, later, Oldknow from Arkwright. But in the early years of the industrial revolution the market for long-term capital was generally local and confined.

Gradually, as the prospects of profit increased, the field of investment widened: men began to lend to enterprises further afield and to industries of which they knew little. In this process a large part was played by merchants, especially those of London, who, accustomed as they were to trust their goods to agents abroad, were often willing to embark part of their resources in industrial concerns at home. The early iron industry of South Wales, for example, was largely the creation of tea-dealers and other traders of London and Bristol, and the Clyde Valley owed much of its industrial equipment to the tobacco merchants of Glasgow. The transmutation of mercantile into fixed capital was an important cause (as well as a result) of the expansion of manufacture.

The industrialist needed not only long-term capital to set up and extend his works, but also working capital to cover the purchase of raw material, the cost of holding the product till it was paid for, and the sums to be handed over periodically to the wage-earners. The first of these short-term needs was generally met by the producer or the dealer—the wool-stapler,

cotton merchant, ironmaster, and so on—who provided th
material on credit which ran into many months and ofte
covered the full period of manufacture. The cost of maintainin
stocks of finished goods, ready for delivery, and of bridgin
the gap between sale and payment was, however, burdensom
Here also long credits were the rule: throughout the eighteent
century it was usually six or twelve months, and sometimes eve
a couple of years or more, before a manufacturer was paid fo
his wares. With the speeding-up of transport and communica
tions there was a tendency to shorten the accommodation; an
the rise in rates of interest that followed the outbreak of th
war with France in 1793 strengthened the practice of giving dis
counts for prompt payment and charging interest on overdu
accounts. A new sense of time was one of the outstandin
psychological features of the industrial revolution.

The payment of wages at more or less regular intervals mear
that the employer had not only to find funds, but find them i
a form acceptable to the wage-earner. Gold guineas, or eve
half-guineas, were of a value too high to be of much use for th
purpose; and, since the currency reforms of 1697 and 1717 ha
left silver undervalued in terms of gold, there was a tendenc
for it to leave the circulation. During the course of the centur
very little silver came into Britain: only small quantities wer
minted, and large amounts of coin were melted down and sen
abroad, by the East India Company in particular. The deart
of coin of small denomination was a serious matter for manu
facturers with wages to pay. Many of them spent days ridin
from place to place in search of shillings. Some effected econo
mies by taking over from the earlier form of industry the prac
tice of the 'long-pay'. And at least one cotton-spinner of th
early nineteenth century met the situation by staggering th
payment of wages. Early in the morning a third of the em
ployees were paid and sent off to make their household pur
chases; within an hour or two the money had passed throug
the hands of the shopkeepers and was back at the factory read
for a second group of workers to be paid and sent off; and i
this way before the day was over all had received their wage
and done their buying-in. Other manufacturers, less ingeniou

or less well-situated, resorted to payment in truck: a practice especially common with those remote from the towns. Others, again, like John Wilkinson and the Anglesey Copper Company, minted their own token coins and paid these to their workers. When, during the Napoleonic War, inflation led to a veritable famine of small change, employers, like Robert Peel and Samuel Oldknow, took to paying wages in bills or small notes which the local shopkeepers were willing to accept on the guarantee of the issuer that he would meet them with a bill on London at a later date. All these practices were objectionable. The abuses to which the truck system was open are obvious: the tokens and shop-notes were often taken by the retailer only at a discount; and wherever wages were paid other than in coin of the realm the employer was in effect shifting his function of providing working capital on to the wage-earners, the shopkeepers, or, where the notes or tokens passed into circulation, the community at large. In many cases, however, he had little or no choice in the matter. The fault lay not, as is sometimes supposed, in cupidity or ill-will on his part, but in defects of the monetary system for which the Government itself was responsible.

If there had been a properly constituted system of banking much of the difficulty might have been avoided. There was, it is true, the Bank of England, which had been set up as early as 1694. But this tended to concentrate its activities on providing accommodation for the State and the merchants and trading companies of the Metropolis, Although in 1708, it had been given a monopoly of joint-stock note issue for England and Wales, it was unwilling to open branches, and hence few of the notes reached the industrial areas. (It was, as has been said, the Bank of London, rather than of England.) There were also in the capital old-established businesses, like those of the Childs and Hoares, which had become merchant banks; but these were concerned mainly with dealings in bullion and foreign exchange, raising loans for governments at home and abroad, and accepting, or guaranteeing, bills of exchange drawn by traders who had opened accounts with them. They too (until 1770) issued notes, but these, like those of the Bank, were

of high denomination and unsuited to the needs of the manufacturers.

For the larger transactions of commerce the instrument was
the bill of exchange, drawn by a creditor on a debtor who ac-
cepted it for payment three, six, or twelve months ahead. Bills
could be passed from hand to hand, and, endorsed by each
holder in turn, gained repute in proportion to the number of
transactions in which they played a part: in Lancashire bills,
often for quite small sums, formed by far the greater part of
the medium of circulation. For payments at a distance, however, it was often necessary that the bill should bear a name with
a reputation in London and so in the country at large. In the
first half of the eighteenth century, and indeed earlier, a country
merchant was often willing, on payment of a commission, to
supply bills, drawn on his London house or correspondent,
to other traders who had payments to make in the Metropolis
or elsewhere. And similarly he was willing to buy, at a discount,
bills which traders or manufacturers had drawn on their customers, and in this way to provide guineas and smaller coin
to those who needed them for the payment of wages or other
purposes. Sometimes he put up on his door a notice that he
was willing to extend these and other facilities to accredited
clients, and so he became a banker.

As far as is known, the first provincial banking house was that
set up, in 1716, by James Wood, a mercer and draper of Gloucester, but it was not until after 1760 that private banks of this
kind became general. They had no common origin. Vaughan
of Gloucester began as a goldsmith, Gurney of Norwich as
a worsted manufacturer, and Smith of Nottingham as a
mercer. In the agricultural districts of England the local corn
merchant often graduated into banking; and in Wales a number of drovers set up at Llandovery an institution known as the
Bank of the Black Ox, and at Aberystwyth another called the
Bank of the Black Sheep (a title which, it should be added, cast
no aspersion on the proprietors, but arose from the fact that
their £1 note bore on it a picture of a black sheep, and their
10s. note one of a black lamb). As manufacture increased, many
industrialists—the Arkwrights, Wilkinsons, Walkers, and the

firm of Boulton and Watt among them—established banks of their own, partly, no doubt, as a means of obtaining cash for wages and bills for remittances, but partly as an outlet for their growing capital. It was from manufacturing sources that Lloyds, Barclays, and other well-known concerns came into being.

By 1793 the country banks numbered about 400, and by 1815 (including some branches) about 900. Each was a relatively small concern, for the law prevented the rise of joint-stock companies; and, even if an Act of incorporation could have been obtained, the privilege granted to the Bank of England made it impossible for any other corporate body to issue notes. Each, however, had a London correspondent bank on which it, or its customers, could draw, and from which notes and coin could be obtained by discounting bills. Some transferred their business to the Metropolis or set up separate banking concerns there, and in this way there arose such well-known London houses as Smith, Payne and Smith, Jones, Loyd & Co., and Taylor, Lloyd and Bowman. In 1760 there had been between twenty and thirty banks in London: by 1800 there were seventy. It was by bankers' drafts on these (bills drawn by one banker on another) that large-scale business was conducted.

When an ordinary bank made a loan to a client it either provided him with a bill or draft, or paid out to him coin, or, more frequently, its own promissory notes. In rural areas, and in most centres of industry other than Lancashire, the notes of the banker became the chief form of money. Against his issue of notes the banker had to keep a reserve of coin, but this was generally small, for if he needed more he could obtain it by sending bills to his agent in London, and the agent, in turn, could replenish his store by sending bills to the Bank of England. All went well so long as the Bank of England was willing to lend freely. But there were occasions when, owing to the overriding demands of the Government or other circumstances, it was obliged to restrict its discounts, and when, therefore, large numbers of local banks were unable to pay out cash, and had to close their doors. The lives of most private banks were short. The fortunes of all were bound up with those of a particular area. Some bankers used the money of depositors for their own trading or speculative purposes. Some were slow to learn what has been called the first lesson of banking—how to distinguish between a bill and a mortgage—and when, as often happened, there was a sudden demand for cash they found themselves with assets locked up in long-term loans. In 1772, 1793, 1814–16, and 1825, in particular, large numbers of them went down, carrying with them to the Bankruptcy Court many manufacturers and traders, and causing loss to all who held their notes.

As time went on it became clear that the small private banks with their limited resources were unable to meet the needs of a factory economy. They were accused of responsibility for the inflation of 1793–1815, and when, in the years of slump that followed the war, large numbers of them failed, they were regarded not merely as the victims, but also as the authors, of the disasters. In the early twenties Thomas Joplin and others pointed out that Scotland, where joint-stock banks were allowed, had been free from financial adversity. And when, in 1826, an inquest was held on the crisis of the preceding year, Parliament decided to permit the setting up of corporate banks in England outside a radius of sixty-five miles of London. The same enthusiasm and local patriotism as had gone to the making of the canals and early railways were brought to the formation of new institutions such as the Manchester and Liverpool District Banking Company, which drew their capital and deposits from a wide field, had many branches, and were able to spread their loans over a variety of industries. At the same time the Bank of England reluctantly yielded to the pressure of Lord Liverpool and began to open note-issuing branches in the provinces. The manufacturers of the thirties and forties had their difficulties to contend with, but a persistent shortage of liquid resources was no longer one of these.

When the Duke of Bridgewater was constructing his canal he drew £25,000 from Child & Co.; when Arkwright was setting up his frames he obtained substantial help from Wright of Nottingham; when, in 1778, Matthew Boulton was heavily involved in engine-building in Cornwall, he had a credit of £14,000 from Lowe, Vere & Co. of London, and shortly afterwards borrowed £2,000 from Elliot and Praed of Truro. In spite of these and many other instances that might be cited, it is doubtful whether the banking system was a principal source of the capital by which the new technique was applied to manufacture. It seems likely that bankers played a larger part in the extension, than in the initiation, of firms, and that the securities they held were mortgages and bonds, rather than shares involving participation in the risks of industry. Common sense alone would have dictated a cautious policy, for the mortality of businesses was high. But the law of partnership was also a determining factor. Large enterprises concerned with public works—turnpikes, canals, docks, bridges, and waterworks—were able to obtain the privilege of incorporation: a banker was often willing to take shares in these, since he had the knowledge that he could dispose of his holding to others if need arose. But Parliament was generally unwilling to concede the same right to manufacturing firms; and, short of becoming a partner, with all that this implied in trouble and risk, there was no way in which the banker could participate in them. He was a creditor rather than a partner of the manufacturer.

The chief contribution of the banks to the industrial revolution consisted in the mobilizing of short-term funds and their transfer from areas where there was little demand for them to others that were hungry for capital. In the agricultural counties landlords, farmers, and dealers paid in to the local banks the bills and cash they received as rent or payment for produce (they were paid interest on the sum deposited or were given interest-bearing notes). The banks remitted the bills to their correspondent bank in London which, after collecting them, found itself with considerable funds. These it used to discount bills for banks in industrial centres, which were thus in turn able to lend to their clients currency, in the form of drafts or bills on London, or cash. The movement took place mainly in the late autumn and early winter, when crops were being sold; but this was the very time when the manufacturers, who settled their accounts at the end of the year, were most in need of funds. The marriage between the thrift of the South and East and the enterprise of the Midlands and the North was both happy and fertile. It meant in effect that rural England was providing foodstuffs for the growing urban communities without requiring an immediate return, and that industrial England was thus able to use its own resources to put up factories and construct canals and railways which benefited manufacturing and agricultural areas alike.

Many institutions besides the banks helped in the process of mustering and distributing capital. In 1773 the Stock Exchange, which had previously consisted of a group of brokers meeting in a coffee-house, obtained premises of its own; its first List, issued in 1803, showed that its dealings were no longer confined to the Funds and East India stock, but covered also public utility and insurance companies. In London there arose specialist bill-brokers, like Richardson, Overend & Co., and finance houses such as those of the Goldsmids, Ricardos, Barings, and Rothschilds; and in the provinces country solicitors increasingly acted as intermediaries for mortgages, annuities, and stock. Insurance (marine, fire, and life) was a powerful instrument for assembling the savings of the middle classes; and those of the workers went largely into friendly societies, the number of which, by 1800, ran into several thousands. From 1798, if not before this, philanthropists, anxious to inculcate a spirit of independence and reduce resort to the parish, had set up savings banks for the working classes: by 1819 there were over 350 of these in various parts of the kingdom, and by 1828 their combined deposits amounted to more than 14 million pounds.

In 1760 Britain was already investing resources abroad, in 'factories' in India, and plantations in the West Indies. But on balance, it seems likely, she was a net importer of capital. Though the long-term rate of interest here had fallen, it was still well above that of Holland, and Dutch bankers and merchants found it profitable to take up investments in England rather than in their own country. Some of them lent direct to English industrialists—in 1769 Matthew Boulton borrowed £8,000 in Amsterdam—but more often they put their money into government, Bank of England, or East India funds. In the middle years of the eighteenth century it was believed that foreigners, mainly Dutch, held about a third of these stocks; and in 1776, according to an estimate (wrongly attributed to Lord North and certainly an exaggeration) about three-sevenths of the British National Debt was in their hands. Foreign capital played a not unimportant role in the early stages of the industrial revolution.

In the course of the American War, however, Holland became involved in hostilities with Britain, and Dutch capital was repatriated. Amsterdam never recovered the loss she suffered at this time, and before the end of the century London had taken her place as the leading centre for international loans. During the wars of 1793–1815 British capital flowed to Europe, as loans or subsidies to allies: there was much investment in the United States and, from 1806, in South America. After 1815 British investors, operating through Barings, Rothschilds, and others, were active in French *rentes* and, as one writer has said, 'all the principal European states found it possible to drown their sorrows by imbibing freely the draught of British capital'. In the early twenties, when rates of interest in this country were low, there was a large efflux of funds to the newly enfranchised colonies of Spain, as well as to Greece. Over the period 1816–25 (according to an estimate made in 1827) Britain lent some 93 million pounds to foreign nations, in addition to smaller amounts invested in mining and trading concerns and carried abroad in the pockets of emigrants.

In 1760 there was nothing that could justly be called a capital market. Lending was still largely a local and personal matter. By 1830 the volume of investable funds had grown beyond measure. Banks, and other institutions, served as pools from which capital, brought by innumerable streams, flowed to industries at home and abroad. Instead of the guess, shrewd or ill-founded, as to the credit-worthiness of the borrower, there was, for part of the field, the published List as a guide. Capital was becoming impersonal—'blind', as some say—and highly mobile.

II

The considerations that led employers to draw people into a single place of work were diverse. In the iron industry the mechanics of smelting and rolling were such that it was virtually impossible to produce on a small scale, and in the cotton industry there was obvious advantage in providing power for a large number of operatives from a single water-wheel or engine. In other cases the reasons were economic rather than technological. On grounds of quality it was essential that the manufacture of chemicals and machinery should be subject to oversight: it was the need for supervision of work that led Peter Stubs to gather the scattered file-makers into his works at Warrington. In the pottery trade the economies to be derived from division and sub-division of labour were the chief inducement to the creation of Wedgwood's Etruria. And in the woollen industry the necessity of putting a stop to embezzlement of material was the main incentive to aggregation in the mills of Benjamin Gott. What is fairly clear is that there was no strong desire on the part of the workers themselves to congregate in large establishments. It was only under the impact of powerful forces, attractive or repellent, that the English labourer or craftsman was transformed into a factory hand.

In the eighteenth century there were many impediments to the movement of labour, whether from place to place or from one occupation to another. Difficulties of transport played only a minor part, for, though the highways might be unsuited to heavy traffic, they were generally good enough for people who travelled on foot. It was not always safe, however, for a man to take to the road, since there were times when he was liable to be picked up by a press-gang, or kidnapped and sent to the Plantations. When James Watt was learning his trade in London in 1756, he was afraid to go abroad in the streets, and when, nearly a quarter of a century later, William Murdoch was sent from Birmingham to Cornwall, it was necessary to provide him with special protection.

More serious were the obstacles that arose from the operation of the Poor Law, and especially from the conditions of settlement. If a man left the parish in which he was domiciled, and remained in another for a full year, he lost his right to relief in the first and established a claim to it in the second. For this reason parish authorities were reluctant to receive outsiders, and employers who were large ratepayers would sometimes offer work only for a period short of a full year. If before a labourer had gained a settlement in a new parish he fell on evil days he could be moved back summarily to the parish from which he had come, and this made him think twice before leaving his native village to seek work far away. After 1795 many parishes in the South, following the policy of the magistrates of Speenhamland, began to give outdoor relief according to a scale based on the price of bread and the size of the family. There was nothing to object to in this: it was only sensible and humane to see that the income of the poor did not fall below the minimum of subsistence. But many of the authorities, confusing the problem of the wage-earner with that of the pauper, undertook to make up from the rates the amount by which the wages of the labourer fell short of their standard. A grant of relief that varies inversely with earnings is the worst form of subsidy, since it destroys the incentive for the worker to demand, or the employer to offer, higher wages. It led to an over-population of the agricultural villages, similar to that which existed on a larger scale in Ireland, and (what is to the present purpose) reduced the pressure on the labourers to move.

Industrial practices inherited from early times were also a deterrent. In corporate towns it was illegal to engage in a skilled occupation without first having served as an apprentice; and, even outside these, most children who wanted to have a trade at their finger ends—and many who had no such aspiration— were bound for six or seven years, and made liable to penalties if they left their employers before the end of the period. Nor was it only the young who were tied in this way. In the coal industry of Scotland all classes of workers were literally serfs, bound by law and custom to a laird, and subject to purchase and sale with the pits; and in Northumberland and Durham, and some other English coalfields, the men were still engaged at annual hirings under bonds which ran just short of the year. One of the biggest problems that confronted the employers of the early years of the industrial revolution was that of selecting men capable of learning the new techniques and susceptible to the discipline that the new forms of industry imposed. When time and energy had been given to this it was only prudent to ensure that the trainee would not be enticed away. Boulton and Watt made their engine-erectors enter into agreements to serve for three or five years; the Earl of Dundonald contracted with one of his chemical workers for twenty-five years; and some of the iron-founders in South Wales were tied for the term of their natural lives.

When an employer sought to engage a man from another district he often failed because he was unable to offer work to other members of the family. To surmount this difficulty iron-masters, like those at Backbarrow, sometimes set up textile works near their furnaces so as to provide employment for the women and children. Conversely, when an employer, like Oldknow or Greg, wanted juvenile or female labour, he was sometimes obliged to extend his operations to agriculture, lime-burning and so on, in order to find work for the men. The industrial unit was often not a single establishment but something approaching a colonial settlement.

The problem can best be illustrated by a survey of employment in the cotton industry. When Arkwright's water-frame thrust its way into a trade organized on a household basis there was much hasty improvization. Early attempts to obtain adult labour proved futile. It had been the practice of many Poor Law authorities to assemble paupers in houses of industry and set them to spinning and other simple tasks; hence it was not unnatural that the new factories should be thought of as workhouses and given a wide berth by the independent labourer. The geographical situation of the mills was such that, in any case, only a small fraction of the labour could be drawn from local sources. It was unthinkable that the male weaver would leave his loom and take to work of less skill as a spinner, and it was equally unthinkable that his wife and children would leave their home for the country factory. But there was, especially in London and the South, a large supply of unskilled, unemployed people who were a charge on the parishes, and in many places the growing burden of the rates led the overseers to offer to transfer batches of children, or whole families, to factories in the North. It was by such means that the cotton masters obtained a large part of their labour.

The story of the factory 'apprentices' is a depressing one. The children, many of them only seven years of age, had to work twelve, or even fifteen, hours a day, for six days a week. As Mr. and Mrs. Hammond said, 'their young lives were spent, at best in monotonous toil, at worst in a hell of human cruelty'. Employers who took their responsibilities seriously—the Arkwrights, the Gregs, Samuel Oldknow, and, above all, Robert Owen—provided not only board in pleasant and well-designed 'prentice houses (such as can still be seen at Styal and Mellor) but also the rudiments of an education. The children were able to play in the fields, and some had little gardens of their own. Care was taken to keep the sexes apart (a visitor to the Cressbrook factory in Millers Dale was told that instruction in singing was given to the boys, but not to the girls, though 'as the girls' rooms were immediately above the boys', the sweet sounds would ascend and the girls participate in the harmony'). Several of the boys at the Gregs' factory at Styal rose to managerial posts, and at least half a dozen of Oldknow's apprentices afterwards set up as spinners on their own account. But at many other places, as at Backbarrow, the tale is one of neglect, promiscuity, and degradation.

When, in 1816, the first Sir Robert Peel was asked about apprentice labour he said: '. . . At the time when Arkwright's machinery had first an existence, steam power was but little known, and . . . those who wished to carry on their business, and benefit by these improvements, resorted to country places where there were great waterfalls, and consequently could not have any other than apprentice labour; and I was in that situation, for I had no other.' A modern might have retorted that he had the alternative of refusing to adopt the new technique at all. But the modern would be passing judgement according

to the code of an age which (because of the industrial revolu
tion) has a standard of life immeasurably higher than that o
Peel's day, and which (partly because children are now in shor
supply) sets a different value on child life. The conduct of th
factory masters must be judged in the light of their own age an
of that which preceded it. It was not very long since Jonas Han
way had remarked that 'few parish children live to be appren
ticed'. Those who did live had been put out to tradesmen an
others, and many had suffered miseries certainly no less thai
those of the factory children. It must be remembered, also, tha
the employers were, like their forbears, essentially merchant
David Dale (we have it on the authority of Robert Owen) di
not visit his factory more than once in two or three months
and the vagueness of the answers that other cotton masters gav
to questions put to them by committees of inquiry arose less
perhaps, from a consciousness that there was something t
hide, than from sheer ignorance of conditions in their ow
works. The superintendents they appointed to their factorie
were largely technicians concerned with the running of th
plant, and the administration of labour was lax. Not until th
industrial revolution was well on its way did there arise a bod
of men capable of performing some at least of the function
of the labour manager of today.

In spite of a widespread impression to the contrary, th
period 1760–1830 saw an increased concern for human unhap
piness, and especially for that of the young—even on the par
of the cotton men. It was Peel who, stimulated by a Mancheste
physician, Thomas Percival, pressed on Parliament the nee
for regulation of the factories. His Act of 1802—the Health an
Morals of Apprentices Act—limited hours of work and pre
scribed minimum standards of hygiene and education. It is tru
that it was passed only when the worst was over, and tha
neither it nor Peel's second Act of 1819 (which applied to al
children, pauper or 'free') went very far. But at least the basi
was laid for that code of legislation which is one of the corner
stones of modern industrial society.

Not all who worked in the country factories were parish ap
prentices. At Arkwright's three mills in Derbyshire, in 178g

about two-thirds of the 1,150 workers were children, but at other establishments, a few years later, the proportion was somewhat lower. For the adults it was necessary to put up houses, shops, and places of worship, and so there arose small communities in which, as time went on, men and women were able, in some measure, to direct their own lives. As the children grew up and had families of their own the practice of drawing on the overseers declined, and the factories came to be staffed by free labour.

The women and children who had spun on the jenny in their own homes found it difficult to compete with the power-driven machines, and, from the early nineties, many began to learn from their menfolk how to weave the calicoes, muslins, and cambrics that were now demanded. At the same time the steam engine and the mule were being applied to the spinning of cotton. The first made it possible to set up factories in the towns, where labour was more plentiful, and the second created a need for a new type of labour in spinning. The mule called for both strength and skill beyond that of a child, and many of the weavers now handed over their looms to their wives and took to factory employment. The occupations of the sexes were reversed, but the family economy remained intact.

As places of work the town factories were no more eligible than those of the country. There was the same dearth of managers and overlookers, and many of the women and children were hired and directed by the male spinners. But the proportion of the very young employed in them was lower than in the water-driven mills of the older pattern. In 1816 at the country factory of Samuel Greg, of a total of 252 workers, 17 per cent were under ten, and not quite 30 per cent above eighteen, years of age. A few miles away in Manchester, M'Connel and Kennedy were giving employment to 1,020 people, of whom only 3 per cent were under ten, and 52 per cent were above eighteen. Even in the town factory, however, it is clear that a large part of the labour consisted of young people. The reliance on workers of tender years was partly the result of technological change and partly of the fact that (as Dr. Ure put it) it was 'nearly impossible to convert persons past the age of

puberty, whether drawn from rural or from handicraft occupations, into useful factory hands'.

In the early decades of the nineteenth century weaving began
to follow spinning and became a factory process. But whereas
the water-twist and mule-spinning factories had sprung up
almost overnight, the power-operated weaving mills came very
slowly. This was due partly to imperfections in the power-loom
itself, partly to the long war with France (which, by raising the
rate of interest, discouraged investment in plant), and partly
to the reluctance of the weavers, many of them women, to leave
their homes. With peace and the falling rates of interest of the
twenties, many master spinners came to attach weaving sheds
to their mills; but it was not until after 1834, when the austerity
of the new Poor Law was brought to bear on the semi-starved
hand-loom weavers, that the full triumph of the factory was assured. As the power-looms increased in number the demand
for domestic weavers declined; but the supply of these was
maintained by an influx of Irish who, content with low standards of living, were even less patient than the English of the
discipline of the factory. It is sometimes suggested that the
'evils' of the industrial revolution were due to the rapidity with
which it proceeded: the case of the domestic textile workers
suggests the exact opposite. If there had been in weaving a man
of the type of Arkwright, if there had been no immigration and
no Poor Law allowance, the transfer to the factory might have
been effected quickly and with less suffering. As it was, large
numbers of hand workers continued, for more than a generation, to fight a losing battle against the power of steam. In 1814
the price paid for weaving a piece of calico by hand had been
6s. 6d.; by 1829 it had fallen to 1s. 2d.

The plight of overworked apprentices and under-employed
domestic weavers does not constitute the full story of the revolution in textiles. It is not necessary to accept as evidence the
picture drawn by the egregious Dr. Ure of the 'lively elves'
whose work in the factory 'seemed to resemble a sport', in
order to believe that, all in all, the effect of the inventions
was to lighten labour. Most of the factory operatives were engaged at rates of pay which raised family incomes above those

of any earlier generation. As women and girls became less dependent on their menfolk they gained in self-respect and in public esteem. As the factories moved to the towns, or towns grew up about the factories, the practice of the long pay gave way to weekly or fortnightly disbursements, and truck and the indebtedness of workers to employers declined. Since the operatives were no longer isolated cottagers it was easier for them to form unions to defend their standards of hours and wages; and it became possible to enlist in the fight against abuses, the force of a public opinion which, through the medium of church and chapel and the Press, was becoming increasingly vocal.

In other industries the course of change, though less spectacular, was similar to that in textiles. In coal-mining, as in cotton-spinning, the central problem was that of obtaining an adequate supply of labour, and many of the devices that were introduced were aimed at enabling boys and youths to do work that had previously been done by experienced pitmen. Some enlightened Scottish owners, including Dundonald and Sir John Sinclair, had liberated their collier-serfs; and, by Acts of Parliament passed in 1774 and 1779, the lifetime bondage of Scottish miners in general was brought to an end. The motive was, no doubt, mainly humanitarian; but some of the employers had supported emancipation by urging that it would raise the status of the coal-getter and so draw into the industry new supplies of labour. Their hopes proved vain. Many of the liberated colliers moved out, some to the ironworks, some to the army, and some to England—though not to the mines of Northumberland and Durham, which were too deep and dangerous to attract the Scots, even if the pitmen had been willing to allow them to come in.

In this northern English coalfield the miners formed a compact, self-contained community. They were prolific, and, since sons almost invariably followed their fathers to the pits, the number of workers increased steadily. But, as the industrial revolution proceeded, and as, with the improvements in transport, markets widened, the demand for coal grew more rapidly than the supply of colliers. The effect was registered in a rise of wages and, even more, in an increase of the premium paid to the pitmen at the annual hirings. During the first half of the eighteenth century this had amounted to only a few shillings, but in 1764 it rose to three or four guineas, and in 1804 (a year of boom) to as much as eighteen guineas, a head. It is to the credit of the pitman that he used his increased income to withdraw his womenfolk from the mines. (There is no recorded instance of women or girls working underground in the northern field after 1780.) But the rise in the wages of the adult miner gave an impetus to the use of boys, who were employed, in increasing numbers, to open and shut the doors that regulated the currents of air, to drag the corves from the face to the main passages, and to drive the ponies along these to the pit bottom.

In the smaller coalfields of England and Wales, where development was slower and pits smaller, less use (so it seems) was made of child labour, but, on the other hand, women continued to work below ground. It is sometimes suggested that the presence of women in an industry has a humanizing effect on the men who work in it; but one would need to take a very optimistic view of the nature of man to believe that this was true of coal-mining. The evils brought to light in the reports of the early forties have sometimes been laid at the door of the industrial revolution, but, like so many other abuses, they went back to a more primitive stage of production, and were, in fact, tending to disappear.

The improvements in spinning, weaving, and mining were broadly of a labour-saving character: they enabled a few workers to achieve results that had previously required many, and children to perform tasks that had formerly been set to men or women. But output was so much enlarged that, in spite of this, the earnings of most of the adults were increased. There were other industries in which progress followed a different course. In engineering (civil and mechanical) and in the manufacture of iron, chemicals, and pottery the problem was that, not of finding semi-skilled labour to tend machines, but of training up men in the new techniques. Much of the time of the inventors themselves was taken up in this way. Brindley had been obliged to begin his task with the aid of miners and common labourers, but in the process of constructing his canals he created new classes of tunnellers and navvies of high skill. In his early days Watt had to make shift with the millwrights— men who could turn from one job to another and were willing to work alike in wood, metal, or stone, but were hide-bound by tradition: before he died there had come into being specialized fitters, turners, pattern-makers, and other grades of engineers. The first generation of cotton-spinners had themselves employed 'clock-makers' to construct and repair their frames and mules; but gradually these were replaced by highly trained textile machinists and maintenance men. Cort's innovations meant that the craftsmanship of the finers and hammermen was no longer required, but they demanded a dexterity no less great from the puddlers and rollermen whom he himself trained. If Wedgwood split up the manufacture of pottery into a score of separate processes, each of these required its own special aptitude, and some a high degree of artistic talent. Nor was this access of skill at the expense of the handicrafts that remained outside the field of large-scale industry. The building of the factories called for proficiency from bricklayers, masons, and carpenters, and their equipment for the craftsmanship of spindle-makers, filesmiths, and a host of others who worked individually or in small concerns. The statement, sometimes made, that the industrial revolution was destructive of skill is not only untrue, but the exact reverse of the truth.

In this group of industries the organization of production was at first even more loose than in the cotton mills. The canals and railways were built by a chain of contractors and sub-contractors who employed gangs of navvies and labourers with little control by the engineer who was responsible for the enterprise as a whole. In the metal trades the journeyman system of sub-letting continued long after the workers had been brought to a common place of employment. In the iron industry the smelters and founders engaged their own apprentices and paid their own labourers. And in the manufacture of pottery (where the typical undertaking was not a factory but a number of workshops grouped together) the boy pressers, turners, and platemakers were indentured to, or hired by, the workmen themselves. Whether the young or unskilled were well or badly treated depended very much on the character of the gang-master or artisan for whom they worked. But since, in most of these occupations, innovation was largely of a capital-saving nature, its effect was to increase not only output but also the share of the value of this that went to the worker. In income, at least, the gain to labour can hardly be in doubt.

As the capital embodied in building and appliances increased, it became a matter of concern to the owners that it should not stand idle unnecessarily. In most occupations hours of work were from dawn to dusk, with short halts for breakfast and dinner. Punctuality in beginning or resuming work was a prime industrial virtue, and the clock, which had a prominent place on the face of the factory, was at once an aid to rectitude and a witness to default. (There is a well-attested story that when the Duke of Bridgewater reproved his men for being late in returning after the midday break they excused themselves by saying that they had failed to hear the stroke of one: the Duke immediately had the clock altered so that henceforth it struck thirteen.) At Etruria, from Lady Day to Michaelmas, the bell rang at 5.45 and work began at six; for the rest of the year it sounded a quarter of an hour before daybreak, and work continued until it was no longer possible to see. But in 1792 William Murdoch demonstrated the possibility of using coal gas as an illuminant, and from the early days of the new century many factories and works were run through the hours of dark. Whether the working time was longer or shorter than that of the domestic craftsman is impossible to say: it can hardly have been longer than that of the nail-workers who (according to Thomas Attwood in 1812) worked from four in the morning till ten at night.

The second generation of employers—such as the sons of Boulton, Watt, Wedgwood, and Crawshay—was perhaps more alive than the first to the losses that might arise from irregularity or carelessness on the part of labour. Men trained in the concern were appointed as managers and foremen; piece-rates and bonus schemes were introduced to stimulate effort; and fines were imposed for drunkenness, sloth, and gaming. The new methods of administration, the new incentives, and the 'new discipline' were as much a part of the revolution as the technical inventions themselves: adaptation to them was the price the workers had to pay for the higher incomes that large-scale industry brought.

The hand-loom weavers, stockingers, nail-makers, and the labourers of the agricultural South, were slow to respond to economic change. And there were others who—whether from inertia, conservatism, or an understandable wish to control their own lives—refused to conform to the new order. They, too, paid their price. But as the rigours of the laws of settlement were relaxed, and as news of the earnings to be made in the factories was spread (by the Press, the town crier, and most often, by ordinary word of mouth), the drift to the rising centres of manufacture increased. The movement of individuals was generally over only a short distance: from the Cheshire countryside to the Lancashire town, from the outlying parts of Staffordshire or Worcestershire to Birmingham, from the Peak district to Sheffield, or from one valley of South Wales to the next. In the areas from which the migrants had gone a shortage of labour caused wages to rise, and hence people from farther afield moved in to these. As Professor Redford has shown, a series of short waves of migration achieved in the end the effect of a long wave, rolling from the South and East to the Midlands and the North.

There was, however, one long-distance movement that was direct. The attractive power of English wages, and the repellent force of hunger—especially in the famines of 1782–4 and 1821–3—brought large numbers of Irish men and women, from their sub-divided holdings, to seek work or subsistence in Britain. Arrived here, some simply swelled the body of paupers; but some took to harvesting, hop-picking, and other forms of agricultural work—and, after having saved a few pounds, declared themselves penniless and got the Poor Law authorities to give them a free passage home. Many, however, remained in Britain. Some were employed in the heavy and less skilled occupations of building and coal-heaving; but the majority made a living by work in textiles, either as spinners at Glasgow and Paisley, or as hand-loom weavers in England. Their Celtic impetuosity, impatience of authority, and gifts of speech, were not without effect on industrial relations (and, in particular, on the character and methods of trade unions) in the later years of the industrial revolution in Lancashire.

The influx of the Irish was offset (and perhaps more than offset) by an exodus of English and Scots overseas. The movement of artisans had been prohibited by a series of statutes aimed at preventing knowledge of British processes from reaching possible competitors in Europe and America; and employers, including Samuel Garbett and Josiah Wedgwood, had been active in prosecuting would-be emigrants and those who tried to seduce them. After 1815, however, the fear of foreign competition abated: it was no longer a shortage, but a surplus of labour, skilled and unskilled alike, that seemed to legislators to constitute the danger. And so, in 1824, the laws prohibiting the emigration of workmen (and the export of machinery) were repealed, and British labour, like British capital, was free to move to any country willing to receive it.

It would be wrong to leave the impression that the growth of the manufacturing population was entirely, or even mainly, the result of increased geographical mobility. There is, indeed, no evidence of any mass exodus from the English countryside to the industrial towns, and it seems likely that the redistribution of labour took place largely in less abrupt ways. Little by little men and women who had previously divided their activities between agriculture and weaving or mining came to work full-time at the loom or the coal face, without moving their households. The tradition that sons and daughters should follow the occupations of their parents was weakening, and so it was possible for factory employment to expand by drawing in more children, and for domestic employment to contract as the number of young entrants fell short of that of the adults who died or retired. But, without proper statistics it is impossible to say how much weight should be attached to each of these tendencies.

What is certain is that by 1830 Britain had, in one way or another, obtained a body of wage-paid workers, acclimatized to factory conditions and able to move from place to place, and from employment to employment, as occasion required. Rates of pay had come to respond more quickly to local changes of demand and supply, and to vary with the upward and downward swings of general activity. Wages in one industry were linked with those in another, and, in particular, the earnings of farm labourers and builders moved up and down with those of the factory operatives. Instead of a number of local and imperfect markets in which men offered their services to a few employers on whose goodwill they depended for work, there was coming into being a single, increasingly sensitive, market for labour.

5

'Individualism' and 'Laisser-Faire'

In the eighteenth century the characteristic instrument of social purpose was not the individual or the State, but the club. Men grew up in an environment of institutions which ranged from the cock-and-hen club of the tavern to the literary group of the coffee-house, from the 'box' of the village inn to the Stock Exchange and Lloyd's, from the Hell Fire Club of the blasphemers to the Holy Club of the Wesleys, and from the local association for the prosecution of felons to the national Society for the Reformation of the Manners among the Lower Orders and the Society of Universal Good Will. Every interest, tradition, or aspiration found expression in corporate form. The idea that, somehow or other, men had become self-centred, avaricious, and anti-social is the strangest of all the legends by which the story of the industrial revolution has been obscured.

It would have been remarkable indeed if, in a community so compact of associations, the industrialist had remained aloof from his fellows. The hedges that were rising about the fields, and the factory walls that enclosed the workers and machines, were not the symbols of a growing individualism but the conditions of a more efficient administration of resources. The firm itself was less often a one-man concern than a partnership, each member of which brought to a common stock his special gift of skill, capital, or knowledge of the market. The partners of one firm were in close, and often daily, contact with those of other firms. They met as worshippers at the same church or chapel, as privates or officers in the same company of Volunteers, as members of the same club of anglers, or as riders or spectators at the same local meet. Many were subscribers to one or other of the bodies which sought to extend to the provinces the activities of the Society of Arts or the Smeatonian Club of London, and in this way they shared (though no doubt to a limited degree) their knowledge of improvements in technique. It is not to be supposed that their corporate endeavours were always, or even generally, directed to beneficent ends. For, as Adam Smith remarked, 'people of the same trade seldom meet together, even for merriment or diversion, but the conversation ends in a conspiracy against the public, or in some contrivance to raise prices'. Many an innocent-looking social or scientific group was, it seems likely, a business organization, the real purpose of which was to blunt the edge of competition and regulate output, prices, wages, or the terms of credit, in some particular trade.

It was in the mining and metal-producing industries that combination reached its greatest height. The coal-owners of the Tyne had for long contrived to keep up the price of fuel in London by limiting the 'vend' and assigning quotas to individual collieries. When the mines of the Wear, and later those of the Tees, were opened up, their proprietors were drawn into the organization; and, with short interludes of open trade, regulation continued till—long after the end of our period— the railways came to the rescue of the consumer with supplies of coal from inland fields. The smaller productive units in metal mining had less economic power. In the middle years of the eighteenth century the copper-miners of Cornwall were, indeed, themselves exploited by the smelters of Bristol and Swansea, who had associated to press down the price of ore. When, however, in the eighties, Thomas Williams began to develop the rich resources of Parys Mountain in Anglesey, the situation of the Cornishmen became so acute that (with the support of Boulton, Watt, Wedgwood, and Wilkinson) they formed a defensive alliance. Like most cartels, the Cornish Metal Company fixed prices at such a high level that output increased and sales declined; and, in spite of an agreement with the Anglesey partners for a division of the market, the accumulation of stocks became so great that, in 1792, the organization broke down. But for the war, which brought large orders from the Admiralty, both Cornwall and Anglesey might have presented, at this early stage, the spectacle of the depressed area with its surplus capacity, unemployed labour, and falling standards of life.

In the iron industry the raw material came from so many scattered sources that it was hardly possible for those who mined it to control the market. But from the early years of the eighteenth century the owners of furnaces in Lancashire and South Wales had been in the habit of fixing the prices both of the charcoal they bought and the pig iron they sold. As the process of smelting with coke developed, the Darbys and the Wilkinsons entered into agreements as to the charges they should make for steam-engine parts; and, before 1777, the ironmasters of the Midlands were holding regular meetings to determine the prices of pig and bar iron and castings. In 1799, on the initiative of Joseph Dawson of Low Moor, the smelters and founders of Yorkshire and Derbyshire set up a similar organization, and, within a short time, there had come into being yet other associations in Scotland and South Wales. During the first decade of the new century these district societies sent delegates to quarterly meetings, representative of the industry as a whole, and until well into the thirties regulation continued on both a regional and a national scale.

At the same time the users, no less than the producers, of copper, iron, and other metals were drawing more closely together. The silver-plate manufacturers of Sheffield, the manufacturers of Birmingham, the file-makers of Warrington and Liverpool, the nailsmiths of Staffordshire, and the pin-makers of Bristol, Gloucester, and other places, each had their own organization. There was, indeed, hardly a single branch of the semi-domestic metal-working trades that was untouched by the tendency to combine.

In industries where the number of firms was large, the variety of products wide, and markets scattered, the exercise of control was less easy. The records of the pottery trade provide instances of agreed price-lists for years as far apart as 1770, 1796, and

1814, and those of the cotton industry give evidence that spinners in Lancashire were accustomed to exchange information on prices with others in Scotland. It was, however, to the breaking down, rather than the setting up, of exclusive privilege, that the efforts of the potters and cotton-men were turned. Led by Wedgwood, they first managed to nullify the monopoly of china clay that had been granted to William Cookworthy and Richard Champion; and, under the guidance of Peel, the second succeeded in obtaining the revocation of the patents of Arkwright. In 1784 both groups joined hands with the ironmasters and the manufacturers of Birmingham to protest against a proposed excise on fustians, coal, and transport. And when, in the following year, Pitt announced his intention of admitting Ireland to the colonial and foreign trade of Britain, they organized the opposition and took the lead in founding a General Chamber of Manufacturers, with Wedgwood as its chairman.

This ambitious project to enable the industrialists to exert pressure on 'the great council of the nation' was destined, however, to reveal cleavages rather than to demonstrate unity. In 1786–7, when Eden was framing his commercial treaty with France, a difference arose between the delegates of the older trades of London and those of the newer industries of the provinces. The manufacturers of silk, ribbons, paper, glass, and leather had experienced no revolution in technique: their chief markets were at home, and their fears were of competition from the foreigner. The men of cotton, iron, brass, and earthenware, on the other hand, were eagerly reaching out to the newly discovered powers of steam: they had little cause for anxiety about imports from France, and their products were already finding outlets abroad. After the signing of the Treaty the debates in the chamber became so acrimonious as to lead Boulton, Garbett, Wilkinson, and Wedgwood himself to withdraw, and it was then only a matter of time for the organization to dissolve.

The plan to set up a federation of British industries was at least a century in advance of the age. After the disappearance of the Chamber the manufacturers made few attempts to intervene in affairs. In 1796, and again in 1806, the ironmasters were successful in opposing the project to put duties on coal and iron. Commercial societies, which sprang up at Manchester, Leeds, Birmingham, Glasgow, and other places, made frequent representations on the obstacles that war and policy put in the way of trade. At a later stage the Chambers of Commerce that grew out of these were to play a significant part in the repeal of the Corn Laws and the institution of Free Trade. But in general the instinct of the industrialists was to eschew politics. It was not by the arts of lobbying or propaganda, but by unremitting attention to their own concerns and their specialized trade organizations, that, after the end of our period, they became a power—perhaps the greatest power—in the State.

The corporate sense of labour, like that of capital, found expression in many forms. The situation of the domestic workers, scattered as these were, was hardly such as to make combination easy. Yet even in the first half of the eighteenth century there was a vigorous growth of clubs among the wool-combers, weavers, tailors, nail-makers, and other craftsmen. Most of these hid their true purposes under titles which implied the activities of friendly societies, and in many respects they were nearer to the gild of early times than to the trade union of today. In trades where almost every adult had his assistant or apprentice the line between employer and workman was not easily drawn. In Lancashire many small employers subscribed to the box, and in Sheffield both masters and men met at an annual candle-light supper, or took wine together at the King and Miller on Saturday nights. In the West Country, however, the planes of cleavage were more sharply defined, and here the course of industrial relations was broken by frequent strikes. But in each of the textile and metal areas the points at issue were much the same. Union activities were directed to the regulation of entries to the trade, to the suppression of 'unfair' workers, and to appeals to authority to give effect to the Elizabethan Acts relating to wages.

As time went on the language of organized labour began

to take on a more strident note, and from 1760 the coalfields, the ports, and the textile villages were often scenes of violence. In 1765, the pitmen of the Tyne, on strike against the introduction of a leaving certificate, cut the winding ropes, smashed the engines, and set fire to the coal underground. In the later sixties jenny riots in Lancashire led to the destruction of machines and houses—and, perhaps, to the flight of Hargreaves and Arkwright to Nottingham. In 1773 the sailors of Liverpool staged a pitched battle in which (as Mr. Wadsworth tells us) they hoisted the 'bloody flag', sacked the houses of the shipowners, and trained cannon on the Exchange. Not all such disturbances, however, are to be taken as evidence of the existence of unions. Some were merely a spontaneous reaction to hunger or oppression, and the organization behind them collapsed as soon as the battle had been lost or won. But in the skilled trades, and among the millwrights in particular, the unions seem to have had a more or less continuous life. Towards the end of the century there was a lusty growth of friendly societies, and it is not without significance that many of these had an occupational basis and that it was in the growing centres of factory production—in Lancashire, Yorkshire, and Lanarkshire—that the development was most marked. The women and children employed in the frame-spinning mills were, it is true, too weak to combine. But in the nineties the men who worked the jennies in the factories, the mule-spinners, and even the hand-loom weavers, had built up strong organizations. Already the sense of a common interest was leading local bodies to federate, and in times of strife men in one industry were beginning to give aid to those in another. By the end of the century trade unionism was no longer a matter of sporadic and temporary association: it was beginning to appear as a movement.

More than two hundred years earlier, the State had made provision for the regulation of labour, and, though the statutes were now rarely enforced, it was held that to seek to increase wages, other than by appeal to the Justices, was illegal or even a crime. So long as a union remained passive it was left undisturbed, but the outbreak of a dispute was often the occasion for the employers to petition for an Act to put down combination in the trade concerned. Before the end of the century the number of such pieces of legislation (not all of which, however, were enforced) exceeded forty; and in 1799 the master mill-wrights of London, at odds with their men, were seeking yet another Act of this kind. Britain was at war: the ruling classes feared that unions might serve as a cloak for 'corresponding societies' or other, more revolutionary bodies. When, there-fore, Wilberforce proposed that the millwrights' Bill should be extended to cover workers in all occupations, opposition was small. The Act of 1799 laid down that any person who joined with another to obtain an increase of wages or a reduc-tion of hours might be brought before a magistrate and, on conviction, sentenced to three months in prison. When it was realized that the magistrate might be an employer, and even a party to the dispute, there were loud protests; and, as a result of these, the measure was superseded by another, not very dif-ferent in substance, in the following year.

The Combination Act of 1800 had been given unwarranted prominence in the histories of trade unionism in Britain. As Mrs. Dorothy George has shown, it was in fact rarely invoked —partly, no doubt, because the penalties it imposed were rela-tively light. In most instances where workers were indicted for combining (as in the famous case of the compositors of The Times in 1810) the action was one for conspiracy under the Common Law, or for breach of some measure relating to a par-ticular trade. The whole apparatus of penal legislation was, indeed, of less effect than might have been imagined. Many unions were formed in the first quarter of the nineteenth cen-tury, and some of these operated in the open, without any action being taken to put them down.

The law of combination applied to employers no less than to workers. No one who has looked at the correspondence of industrial concerns of the period can have any doubt that the masters were often guilty of infringing it. Yet there were few, if any, prosecutions for conspiracy to force down wages. The difference of attitude in the two cases could not fail to im-press itself on fair-minded men, and especially on those who were imbued with the doctrines of Adam Smith and Jeremy

Bentham. Francis Place (1771–1854), the tailor of Charing Cross, who had himself suffered in early life from the austerity of the law, took up the cause of the trade unions. Aided by Joseph Hume, he succeeded, in 1824, in obtaining the removal of the disabilities of the workers under the Common and Statute law of combination. Immediately large numbers of unions that had lived underground came into the open. New societies were formed, and, since 1824 was a year of prosperity and mounting prices, many claims were put forward for advances in wages. All this led to second thoughts on the part of the politicians. A Bill was brought in, and passed in 1825, which, though it confirmed the legality of combination, imposed penalties on workers who might be found guilty of molesting, obstructing or intimidating others. It was left to the Courts to determine, over long years to come, what was meant by each of these ambiguous terms.

The four or five years of falling prices that followed the collapse of the boom of 1825 were unfavourable to trade union activity, and most of the strikes of this period failed in their objects. In the early thirties, under the leadership of John Doherty and Robert Owen, schemes were advanced for the amalgamation of societies and the formation of a single Grand National Consolidated Trades Union. The idea was as premature as that of the industrialists, half a century before, for a General Chamber of Manufacturers. It was not by a sudden creation of this kind, but by a painful process of laying brick upon brick, that the national unions, as we know them today, were built up.

Not all the 'industrious poor' were able to organize their own defences. There were many who, because of low earnings, unemployment, disease, or misfortune, were forced to rely upon charity. If the period gave rise to much that was ugly and squalid it also threw up men and women, such as Jonas Hanway, Elizabeth Fry, and William Wilberforce, narrow, it may be, in creed, but wide in compassion. Most of the industrialists were too much wrapped up in their own adventures to be active in social reform. But there were some, like Richard Reynolds of Coalbrookdale, who were renowned for philanthropy; and the letters of others give evidence of more altruism than the text-books would have us believe. Nor were the politicians altogether insensitive to social abuses. The governments that passed measures 'for preventing the excessive use of spirituous liquors', for regulating the employment of poor-law apprentices, for abolishing serfdom in the coalfields of Scotland, and for suppressing the slave trade, were not just the instruments of a class devoid of humanity.

Generally, however, alleviation was the business, less of the individual or the State, than of the voluntary organization. Public relief was supplemented by bodies like the Society for Bettering the Condition of the Poor, the Marine Society, which provided for friendless boys, and the Philanthropic Society, which cared for deserted children and vagrants. One kind of distress was met by the Royal Humane Society ('for the recovery of persons existing in a state of suspended animation'). Another was the concern of the Society for Improving the Condition of the Infant Chimney-Sweepers. Yet another was the responsibility of the Society for the Relief of Persons Imprisoned for Small Sums. Education was the province of the Society for the Propagation of Christian Knowledge, of the charity schools, and, later, of the Lancasterian and National organizations. And what is sometimes described as 'the' social evil was the special field of the Society for Enforcing His Majesty's Proclamation against Vice. Some of these bodies confined their activities to the Metropolis, but there were others that grew up in the provinces to deal with the problems of industry and the new town: the Manchester Board of Health, in particular, was a pioneer of sanitary and factory reform.

If it cannot be held that the period of the industrial revolution was one of individualism—at least in the narrow sense of the term—it may with some justice be maintained that it was an age of *laisser-faire*. This unhappy phrase has been used as a missile in so many political controversies that it now appears battered and shabby. But there was a time when it was employed, not as an epithet of abuse, but as an inscription on the banners of progress.

The belief that the Tudors and Stuarts had a consistent plan for the conduct of economic relations dies hard. The regulation of wages, employment, technical training, industrial location, prices, and commerce established by them was, in fact, less generous, less enlightened, and less systematic than is sometimes supposed. However that may be, the diminution of the powers of the Crown and the weakening of the Privy Council in the seventeenth century meant that some at least of the instruments of control were allowed to rust. At the same time the rise of wider markets, more elaborate techniques, and more specialized types of labour, must have made the task of detailed supervision difficult indeed. Even if there had been no Civil War, no Glorious Revolution, and no rise of new classes to political power, central direction must almost certainly have broken down. For more than a hundred years before the industrial revolution the State was in retreat from the economic field.

There were points, indeed, at which it still clung to the lines of its earlier front. There were still authoritative corporations—trading concerns like the East India Company, and regulative bodies like the Cutlers' Company of Hallamshire—that owed a continuance of their powers to a grant from the Crown. And the whole field of foreign commerce, navigation, and imperial economic relations was subject to state interference. A series of economic writers and publicists had attacked the outworks of the system. In 1776 Adam Smith turned his batteries on a crumbling structure, and through his influence on Pitt and, later, on Huskisson and others, some breaches were made in the ramparts. *The Wealth of Nations* gave matchless expression to the thoughts that had been raised in men's minds by the march of events. It gave logic and system to these. In place of the dictates of the State, it set, as the guiding principle, the spontaneous choices and actions of ordinary men. The idea that individuals, each following his own interest, created laws as impersonal, or at least as anonymous, as those of the natural sciences was arresting. And the belief that these must be socially beneficial quickened the spirit of optimism that was a feature of the revolution in industry.

Experience has taught us, however, that an industrial society needs a framework of public services if it is to operate without social discomfort. Some of Adam Smith's followers, intoxicated by the new doctrine, were disposed to confine the role of the State to defence and the preservation of order: *laisser-faire* was extended from the economy to society at large. The extremists were strengthened by the teaching of Thomas Malthus, whose *Essay on Population* appeared when the industrial revolution was in full stream; and here again the disciples failed to observe the qualifications that the master had made. If people always tended to grow in numbers as the means of subsistence increased there could never be a raising of standards for the mass of mankind: to give charity was only to pour oil on the flames. The pessimism of Malthus, no less than the optimism of Smith, may have directed many to the comfortable position of leaving everything alone. But fortunately most Englishmen have too much good sense to walk by the light of abstractions, and the actions of men, as this chapter has shown, were often better than their creeds or their theories.

With the best will in the world, the transition from farms and cottages to factories and cities could never have been smooth. If the legislative machine had turned out statutes with the same speed as the mules turned out yarn there would still have been social disorder. For much of the overcrowding and squalor was the result of the fact that progress in science was then, as today, more rapid than that in administration. 'The remote influence of arrangements has been somewhat neglected', wrote Dr. Kay in 1832, adding to this meiosis that the neglect arose 'not from want of humanity, but from the pressure of occupation and the deficiency of time'. Experience under the Factory Acts of 1802, 1819, and 1831 proved that until a body of inspectors had been trained it was little use to lay down minimum conditions of hours and work. The experience of boards of health showed that until there was a larger supply of medical men and other professional experts not very much could be done to improve conditions in the towns. Colquhoun and others might inveigh against the multiplicity of officials, but the Civil Service was, by modern standards, microscopic, and local services hardly existed at all. Not until the whole apparatus of government had been drastically reformed and a body of qualified public servants had been called into being could life in urban areas be other than squalid. If the industrial revolution was not able to bring its rewards in full measure to the ordinary man and woman it is to the defects of administrative, and not of economic, processes that the failure must be ascribed.

6

The Course of Economic Change

THE industrial revolution is to be thought of as a movement, not as a period of time. Whether it presents itself in England after 1760, in the United States and Germany after 1870, or in Canada, Japan, and Russia in our own day, its character and effects are fundamentally the same. Everywhere it is associated with a growth of population, with the application of science to industry, and with a more intensive and extensive use of capital. Everywhere there is a conversion of rural into urban communities and a rise of new social classes. But in each case the course of the movement has been affected by circumstances of time and place. Many of the social discomforts that have been attributed to the industrial revolution in Britain were, in fact, the result of forces which (for all we know) would still have operated if manufacture had remained undeveloped and there had been no change of economic form.

Among these was the movement of prices. In the first half of the eighteenth century wholesale prices in England were steady, with a slight inclination to fall. Between the middle fifties and the early nineties they rose by some 30 per cent, and between 1790 and 1814 they roughly doubled. From this point there was a fall, swift at first, then more gradual, until in 1830 a level was reached slightly below that of 1790, and less than half that of 1814. For some of these fluctuations responsibility must, indeed, rest with the industrial revolution. For it was of the essence of this that resources should be turned from the making of consumers' goods to that of industrial equipment, and the transfer could hardly have taken place without some alteration of values. After 1760 a larger proportion of the labour force of Britain came to be employed in constructing roads, canals, harbours, ships, factories, and machines, and a smaller proportion in producing food and drink, boots and clothes, furniture and houses. It might be thought that, in due course, the new instruments would have led to a greater output of finished commodities, and that the prices of these would have fallen. But economic processes were frustrated by political adventures; and it was not until the last fifteen years of our period that the industrial revolution could yield its harvest in the form of a more abundant supply of goods for the ordinary consumer.

Although throughout the eighteenth century the volume of silver coin turned out by the Mint was small, that of gold was growing, and the total amount of metallic money almost certainly increased. Banks and business men, moreover, were active in creating a currency of notes and bills: after 1797, this rose to large, and indeed to inflationary, proportions, and the expansion of the National Debt provided a vast supply of securities, which served some, at least, of the functions of money. Naturally, prices moved strongly upward. From 1815, however, the Government and the Bank began to reduce the circulation; during the depression of 1816–17 many country banks were forced to close their doors, and there was a sharp drop in the level of prices. In the twenties the import of precious metals from South American mines failed to keep pace with European needs; and the conditions under which the gold standard was established in 1821 called for a continued contraction of paper. At a time when the output of goods was increasing, the supply of money remained constant or declined, and in these circumstances prices could hardly do other than fall. Conditions outside Britain were also influential. During the war imports had been high in price relative to exports. When it was over a substantial lowering of the cost of imported raw materials and foodstuffs (cotton, wool, sugar, tea, and so on) made a major contribution to the fall in the general level of prices.

Rising prices are frequently associated with expansion, and falling prices with contraction, of activity. It would be wrong, however, to think of the period from 1760 to 1814 as one of unbroken prosperity, or of that from 1815 to 1830 as one of continuous depression: each was marked by ups and downs, some at least of which, again, proceeded from causes independent of technological or industrial change.

For centuries economic life had been dominated by the yield of the soil, and even after Britain had become largely industrialized the state of the crops was a matter of perennial anxiety. Throughout the first half of the eighteenth century the harvests had generally been good, but there had been times when (as in 1709–10, 1727–8 and 1739–40) adverse weather for two seasons in succession had brought a sharp upward movement of the price of bread. Since the greater part of the expenditure of the poor was on food, a bad harvest was necessarily followed by distress. That it must also have been followed by industrial depression is not, at first sight, clear; yet many contemporary observers—from the Lancashire rhymester, Tim Bobbin, to the Scottish economist, Adam Smith—assert quite plainly that dearness of food led to falling wages and lack of work. It is obvious that when ordinary people were forced to spend more on bread they would have less left over to buy clothes and other commodities. But it is no less obvious that the farmers and landlords would find their incomes correspondingly enlarged. It would not be unreasonable to hold that increased expenditure by these would offset decreased expenditure by the rest of the community, and that the state of industrial activity should, therefore, have remained unchanged. Apart, however, from the fact that the relatively well-to-do landlords and cultivators would not want the same goods as the poor, it is doubtful whether very much of their fortuitous profit would be spent at all. Evidence from many different times and places suggests that as income increases the proportion that is hoarded tends to rise. And if this is true of mankind in general it is especially true of the man of the soil; for, as William Cobbett (who knew him) said, the farmer's maxim 'is to keep the money that he takes as long as he can'. It was because the purchasing power that came to the cultivator trickled so slowly through his closed fingers that periods of poor harvests (such as 1756–7, 1767–8, 1772–5, 1782–3, 1795–6, 1799–1801, 1804–5, 1809–13, and 1816–19) were usually followed by stagnation of trade, falling wages, and unemployment.

Government policy was directed to keeping agricultural prices at a level high enough to make farming profitable. By a series of measures the growers of grain were protected against competition from overseas; and under the Corn Bounty Act of 1689 (which remained in force until 1814) there was a subsidy of 5s. on each quarter of wheat exported, so long as the price at home did not exceed 48s. It is true that in years of dearth exports were generally prohibited, and imports allowed in duty free. But, though such expedients did something to relieve hunger, they could not prevent a bad harvest from having at least some adverse effects upon industry. For the decline in the value of exports, and the increase in the value of imports, often led to a fall in the rate of exchange, and hence to a contraction of credit and depression of trade. No fiscal device, however ingenious, could eliminate the effects of the harvests. It was not until Britain had become a creditor nation, with overseas assets to absorb the shock, that a deficiency in the current balance of payments could be looked on without grave concern.

According to Mr. Fussell, during the eighteenth century the area of land under wheat was enlarged by about a third, and the yield per acre raised by about a tenth. But the growth of population was such that, after the middle of the 1770s, Britain ceased to be an exporter and became, in most years, an importer of grain. Nor was it only for cereals that she was coming to rely on the foreigner. Many other articles of diet, like tea and sugar, were brought from abroad, as well as such raw materials as cotton, flax, wool, silk, and timber. For markets also, especially those of the textile and hardware trades, the people of Britain now looked overseas. From 1760 to 1785 there had been a moderate expansion in the annual volume of exports; but as the industrial revolution gathered momentum, sales to foreign countries, and especially to those of Europe, increased in spectacular fashion. If imports of grain did something to

allay one source of instability, this growing reliance on international trade brought with it another; and, from the middle
of the eighties, the earnings and employment of a far larger
number of English workers than ever before came to depend
on what was happening abroad. The prosperity of 1792, 1799,
1802, 1809–10, 1815, and 1824–5 was largely connected with
a rise, and the depression of 1793, 1811, 1816, 1819, and 1826
with a fall, of export demand. Sometimes the turn from boom
to slump was sudden; and the close connections of London
houses with financial institutions abroad meant that an adverse
wind, blowing from Europe or America, not infrequently pre-
cipitated a crisis.

At the same time pulsations of investment at home gave rise
to fluctuations of employment. When money was cheap and
hopes of profit ran high, enterprising men set labour to work
in creating industrial plant or building up stocks of materials;
and since those engaged in these tasks had larger incomes to
spend, firms that made goods for consumers shared in the
prosperity. After a time, however, the increased demand for
funds forced up rates of interest: expectations of profits
fell, and the process of investment was checked. It is not to
be supposed that a rise in the market rate of interest reacted
at once on the ordinary manufacturing concern. As we have
seen, the typical cotton-spinner or ironmaster was largely self-
financing: he put back into his business all he could spare,
without taking much thought of immediate returns. But to
agriculture, building, and works of construction, a change in
the price of money was of vital importance. Since bricks were
used extensively, not only in the erection of houses and factories, but also in the sinking of mines and the making of canals
and bridges, the variations of the numbers produced give an
indication of changes of activity over a wide field. As Mr.
Shannon showed, the output of bricks rose and fell (about a
year later) as the rate of interest moved down or up. And since
higher or lower earnings in one part of the economy led to corresponding movements elsewhere, conditions of well-being,
or those of adversity, became general. When a period of activity
in construction coincided with good harvests and large exports

(as in 1792, 1810, and 1815) there was high prosperity, and when none of these conditions existed depression was deep.

The oscillations of employment were often caused, and still more often magnified, by political forces: over much of the period of the industrial revolution Britain was at war. In some important respects, the men of the eighteenth century were more civilized than those of today: a state of hostilities did not put an end to intercourse between individual Britons and Frenchmen; and, since governments had not yet learnt how to control the lives of their subjects, warfare was never what we now call total. The losses of men and ships were serious indeed, but, these apart, physical destruction was small. It was through the distortion of the economic system, and the disturbance of social relations, that the most serious loss was sustained.

The war of 1756–63 resulted in a rise of prices and interest, a fall of real wages, and an over-stimulation of shipbuilding and the manufacture of iron. It was the seed, moreover, of the dispute with the colonies, which had adverse effects on commerce, and which led to the disaster of 1775. The eight years that followed the outbreak of war with the Americans brought a serious fall of both imports and exports—the only long-sustained decline of the century. They were marked also by a rise in the rate of interest, and by a decrease of investment at home: it was not until 1792, on the eve of a yet greater conflict, that the yield on Consols was back at the level of 1775. In the years of peace of the late eighties, however, there was much activity in building and public works; and 1792 presented all the symptoms of a boom. Early in the following year the demand for workers was such that farmers in various parts of the country asked Parliament to prohibit the employment of labourers in cutting canals during the months of harvest; and, in the light of what we now know of the trade cycle, it is clear that a recession was near.

The outbreak of hostilities with France in this year was the occasion of a crisis the essential feature of which (as of all financial crises) was an acute shortage of cash. Fearing for the future, men hoarded their money; merchants were unable to obtain remittances from abroad, or to continue credits to their clients at home; there was a run on the banks, and many houses that were far from insolvent went down for want of coin and notes. The situation was met by a loan from the Government to merchants, in the form of Exchequer bills, and within a short space of time normal dealings were restored. Very soon, however, it was the turn of the Government to be embarrassed by lack of resources. Loans were raised from the public and the proceeds spent, to a large extent overseas. The cost of maintaining the armed forces abroad, and the need to transmit a large loan to the Austrian ally, led to a fall in the rate of exchange. After the disastrous experiment with the *assignats*, France had restored a gold standard, and balances that had been held for safety in London were now being repatriated. So great was the drain of coin and bullion that in 1797 it was necessary to relieve the Bank of England of the obligation of meeting its notes in gold. After the suspension of cash payments there was no compulsion on either the Bank itself or the country banks to exercise restraint in the discounting of bills, and so, in time, the volume of the currency expanded, and the level of prices was raised. By 1810 it was plain that sterling had fallen in value in terms not only of goods, but also of foreign currencies and gold. There was much debate then, and there has been more since, as to whether the responsibility for the inflation lay with the Bank of England or the private banks. In fact, it lay with the Government, which by borrowing, and spending the proceeds, raised the money income of the public out of proportion to the volume of goods available for civilian consumption. Some measure of inflation, it is now generally recognized, is necessary to the conduct of war. If statesmen had followed the advice of Francis Horner and his colleagues of the Bullion Committee of 1810, and had returned to gold at this time, there would have been a fall of prices so great as to put many people out of work and endanger the prosecution of the war. As it was, the rise of prices increased profits, and, since wages limped slowly behind the cost of living, the standard of life of the workers was lowered.

Government borrowing had another, no less important

effect. In 1792, when Britain was at peace, the yield on Consols had been 3·3: five years later it had reached 5·9. Many projects set on foot when money could be obtained at, or near, the first of these rates could not be continued when the cost of borrowing was raised. Capital was deflected from private to public uses, and some of the developments of the industrial revolution were once more brought to a halt. Expenditure on men-of-war, munitions, and uniforms gave a stimulus to shipbuilding, to the manufacture of iron, copper, and chemicals, and to some branches of the woollen industry. But the progress of the cotton, hardware, pottery, and other trades suffered a check. In the first phase of the war, building was greatly curtailed, but the peace of 1801–3 brought a revival, and between 1804 and 1815 construction (though not that of houses) was maintained at a fairly high level.

Foreign trade also suffered less than in earlier wars. After a fall in 1793, exports mounted, with little setback, to a peace-time boom in 1802. The renewal of hostilities was marked by a decline; but for six years the volume of trade was not unsatisfactory, and in 1809–10 there was, once more, a boom. The attempt of Napoleon to bring Britain to her knees by cutting off her markets was a failure. Direct exports to western Europe, indeed, fell away. But the islands of Heligoland and Malta became spearheads by which British trade penetrated to the heart of the Continent, and there was a growth of exports to the West Indies, the United States, and South America. When in 1810, however, Austria was forced to make peace, and Holland was annexed by the French, some of the channels of commerce were closed; and when, in the following year, the Non-Intercourse Act put a stop to trade with the United States, the volume of British exports fell sharply. But the entry of Russia to the conflict in 1812 brought Napoleon's Continental System to an end; and, in spite of the naval war with America, overseas trade remained good in 1813 and 1814 and rose to a peak at the end of the struggle.

Britain had for long offered warehousing facilities for goods in transit from one country to another. During the war it became a major aim of policy to deflect the merchandise of the

French West Indies, in particular, to London, and then to re-ship it to Europe and elsewhere. In 1790 about 26 per cent of Britain's exports consisted of goods of foreign origin: by 1800 the percentage was 44, and in 1814 it was still as high as 36. It would be wrong, therefore, to infer that a high level of gross exports meant that all was well with the industries that looked for their markets abroad. The condition of the cotton opera-tives and nail-makers, in particular, fluctuated with each change in the fortunes of battle and each shift in the tactics of statecraft. But, on the whole, Britain rode through the storm with her people at work: the price of wars for the civilian is often paid less when they are in progress than when the fighting has ceased.

In April 1814 Napoleon surrendered his throne and was banished to Elba. For several months British industry was borne on a rising wave of optimism: the rate of interest fell, there was a drop in the price of bread, and both exports and production for home markets were high. But before the end of 1815 the boom had broken. Demobilization threw some 300,000 men on the labour market at a time when industry had not yet adjusted itself to conditions of peace. (The records of the Poor Law are eloquent of the fate of many of these.) Euro-pean demand for British goods had fallen off, and Government expenditure had been cut by a half. Merchants and industrial-ists were oppressed by the knowledge that, sooner or later, the monetary standard was to be restored at a parity that could be maintained only if prices were lowered. Private investment was at an ebb and unemployment was widespread. Poor harvests in 1816 and 1817 caused food prices to rise and the demand for manufactured goods to fall. In 1818, indeed, conditions improved. Low rates of interest, revived Government expendi-ture, better harvests, livelier markets abroad, and a raised level of construction at home brought a brief boom. But the three following years were less favoured; and it was not until 1821 that the era of inactive capital and unemployed labour—the era of what we now call reconversion and deflation—was brought to an end.

The experiences of these years have clouded for many the

true nature of the technical and economic changes of the period. Just as the war had thwarted the purpose, so the conditions in which peace was restored postponed the fulfilment, of the revolution in industry. There was, there can be no doubt, alongside the distress, a growth of class feeling and bitterness. Much of this arose, less from a conflict between capital and labour, than from an opposition of views as to where the burden of increased taxation should lie. A Parliament representative largely of landlords demanded the repeal of the income tax, which had been imposed as a war measure, and the introduction of increased duties on grain. It was submitted, not without reason, that the agricultural classes already bore, through the land tax, the tithes, and the poor rates, the greater part of the cost of the public and ecclesiastical establishments. And it was urged, with less justice, that the political services which the landowners rendered entitled them to special consideration from the State. The Corn Law of 1815, which prohibited the release to the millers of wheat from abroad so long as the price at home was below 80s. a quarter, was intended to preserve for the agriculturists a structure of prices and rents that had been created by war—at a time when manufacturers were being forced to sell their products more cheaply, and when money wages tended to fall. In fact, the domestic price of wheat rarely reached 80s. The defect of the law was not that it maintained a consistently high level of prices for grain, but that, in times of dearth, it prohibited relief from abroad until conditions approached those of famine.

Apart from this fiscal injustice, the workers had grounds for complaint. Some, instructed by Tom Paine and William Cobbett, resented their lack of political status, and many had learnt by experience of the limits the law of combination imposed on their bargaining strength. Throughout the eighteenth century, riots had been endemic: again and again the pitmen and sailors, shipwrights and dockers, and the journeymen of the varied trades of London downed tools, smashed windows, and burnt effigies of those with whom they were at variance. About many such incidents there had been something of the light-heartedness of the May Day demonstration. But the tumults of the second decade of the nineteenth century sounded a deeper and more disturbing note. Those who took part in them were not, in the main, factory operatives, but workers who belonged to the older system of industry: the croppers of Yorkshire, the frame-work knitters of Nottingham, and the hand-loom weavers of Lancashire. Under-employed and under-fed men were not over-nice in theorizing as to the cause of their distress, and it was natural enough that they should strike at the machines that appeared to be taking the bread from their mouths. Some of the unemployment was, indeed, the result of technical change; but the chronology of revolt points to the real cause of the trouble. It was 1811, and again in 1816, when political events and bad harvests had led to depression, that the Luddites destroyed the stocking-frames in the Midlands and the power-looms in the North. It was in 1817 that the hungry and workless Blanketeers set off on their dismal march from Ardwick Green in Manchester. And it was in 1819, when, once again, bread was scarce and trade at a low ebb, that the working-class Reformers of Lancashire gathered, and suffered, at St. Peter's Field. The story of repression—of the Home Office spies and the ill-famed Six Acts—has been told too often to bear repetition here. Frightened politicians and an inept administration were not the least of the misfortunes of these unhappy years.

In the early twenties many circumstances combined to produce high prosperity. The currency was established on a foundation of gold and there was a run of favourable harvests. Huskisson and his colleagues were active in pulling down tariffs, lowering excise duties, and removing restrictions from industry and trade: the policy of reform by repeal was good in the eyes of men who had been irked by controls and who asked only to be let alone. A substantial part of the National Debt was converted from 5 to 4 or $3\frac{1}{2}$ per cent: in 1820 the yield on Consols had been 4·4; by 1824 it was 3·3. In 1822 Bank rate, which had stood for almost half a century at 5, was brought down to 4. But Bank rate was not yet a mirror of market conditions, and in the early months of 1825 short-term loans were being placed at little more than $2\frac{1}{2}$ per cent. In Lancashire and

Scotland factories were run up at unprecedented speed, and between 1821 and 1825 the output of bricks more than doubled. Ironworks were busy producing piping for gas and water undertakings and sections for bridges and railways. Stocks of cotton, wool, and other raw materials were built up. Overseas trade expanded; and, since re-exports now constituted only 16 or 17 per cent of the goods sent abroad, the growth was almost entirely the outcome of increased productivity of industry. Canning's recognition of the emancipated colonies of Spain, in 1823, gave a fillip to foreign investment: Latin America seemed to offer boundless opportunities for trade, and the export of capital to this area played a large part in the boom.

High expectations of profit led to a burst of speculative schemes in 1825: many of these were bogus, and others, inherently sound, failed to yield returns as fully, or as promptly, as had been hoped. Since incomes and prices had risen, the exchanges took a downward turn, and there was an almost simultaneous internal and external drain of gold. Correctives were applied. Interest rates were raised and credit was contracted: prices fell and unemployment became widespread. It is unnecessary to detail the story of the depression of 1826, the recovery of 1827, the prosperity of 1828, and the gloom and agricultural distress of 1829 and 1830. The cyclones and anticyclones of the twenties were of the same nature as those that were to pass over England many times in the following decades of the nineteenth century.

It was through such changing seas that the captains of the industrial revolution steered their courses. Many of the difficulties they encountered were, it is clear, of their own making. Some of the navigators were unable to distinguish a false wind from a true, and not all knew when it was safe to clap on sail, or prudent to shorten it. Not all, again, took sufficient thought of the state of their crews: pioneers have often suffered disaster by reason of this. But the major troubles arose, not from want of skill or want of heart—certainly not from want of courage— but from the forces of Nature and the currents of political change. If harvests had been uniformly good; if statesmen had directed their attention to providing a stable standard of value and a proper mediun of exchange; if there had been no wars to force up prices, raise rates of interest, and turn resources to destruction, the course of the industrial revolution would have been smoother, and its consequences would not have been, as they are, in dispute.

Some of these consequences, it must be admitted, were baleful. In spite of the efforts of Thomas Percival and James Watt, the skies over Manchester and Birmingham grew dark with smoke, and life in the cities became drab. The smaller industrial town, like Oldham or Bilston, had a harsh countenance: towns, to be good, should grow slowly. There was, it seems likely, a decline of taste—as the very letterpress of the books to which the student goes for his data bears witness. But all was not loss. The face of England is patient of modulation: enclosing landlords and planters gave it new grace. Nor were the early industrialists insensitive to the appeal of the country: the beauty of Cromford and Millers Dale suffered little by the enterprise of Arkwright, and stretches of the Goyt and the Bollin owe something to Oldknow and the Gregs. Even the products of manufacture are not to be thought of as wholly uncomely: Telford's Anglesey bridge and the pottery of Wedgwood and Spode cry out against that. If large-scale industry overshadowed art and craftsmanship, it did not by any means destroy them.

Much has been written about the effects of the industrial revolution on the workers. Some, impressed by the lot of those who went down in the struggle against the machine, have declared that technological change brought little but misery and poverty, and a statistician of repute has set on record his opinion that by the early years of the nineteenth century the standard of life of the British worker had been forced down to Asiatic levels. He can hardly have looked at the statistics which more than a generation of research has produced. The careful studies of Mrs. Gilboy indicate that, over the eighteenth century, the material well-being of the labourer in the woollen area of the South-West had, indeed, fallen, but that the lot of his fellow in the textile region of the North had steadily improved, and that the labourer of London more than held his own. It is true that the rise of prices after 1793 made many humble people poorer. But before the end of the war (as Professor Silberling has shown) industrial wages in England caught up with retail prices, and in the twenties the gain was maintained. In 1831 the cost of living was 11 per cent higher than in 1790, but over this span of time urban wages had increased, it appears, by no less than 43 per cent.

It would have been strange, indeed, if the industrial revolution had simply made the rich richer and the poor poorer. For the commodities to which it gave rise were not, in general, luxuries, but necessaries and capital goods. The tardiness with which the last of these yielded their fruit to the consumer has already been mentioned. But by the twenties the effects of the war were passing away and the cottons and woollens, and food and drink, which now became available, were consumed not by the few, but by the masses. Some of the products of the factories and ironworks were sent abroad, but the return cargoes did not consist in the main of wines and silks, but of sugar, grain, coffee, and tea for the people at large. Much has been made of the suggestion that the prices of the things Britain exported fell more rapidly than those of the things she brought back: there was no revolution to reduce costs in overseas agriculture; and British lending abroad may also have helped to give the terms of trade an unfavourable turn. But, though such influences may explain why, in the twenties, real wages were lower than might have been expected, they had little effect, it would seem, thereafter. The diet of the worker almost certainly improved: there was a substitution of 'flower of wheat' for rye and oatmeal; and meat, which had been a rarity, became, with potatoes, the staple dish on the artisan's table. Not all the coal raised from the pits went to feed the furnaces and steam-engines: a warm hearth and a hot meal were of no small consequence to the man who came home wet from the fields.

In 1802 George Chalmers remarked that the laborious classes were 'too wealthy to covet the pittance of the soldier, or too independent to court the dangers of the sailor'. There were, true enough, many vagrants and paupers, but, even before the new Poor Law came in, the hordes of the 'indigent and distressed' had probably shrunk. Hours of labour were long, and holidays few; there is a mass of evidence that employment in factories was harmful to the health and morals of the young. A leading politician has recently spoken of the 'mechanized horrors of the industrial revolution', and there can be little doubt that the deeper mines and more complicated machines brought new risks of mutilation and death. But against all this must be set the lessening of strain on those who worked in the heavy trades, and the decline in the number of crippled and deformed people that followed the introduction of power in places like Sheffield. There must be set, also, the reduction of sweating of women and young children, the rise in family earnings, the greater regularity of pay, and the gain in welfare that came as industrial work was taken out of the home.

Whether the houses themselves were becoming better or worse is difficult to determine: much depends on the periods compared. Many of the dwellings provided for the workers by the country factory masters have survived—at Cromford, Mellor, and Styal. They have design and proportion, and, even by modern standards, are not wanting in amenity and comfort. But these were put up when building materials were plentiful, wages relatively low, and money relatively cheap. After 1793 the import of timber from the Baltic was restricted, and the price of labour of bricklayers and carpenters went up. At least two-thirds of the rent of a dwelling consists of interest charges: rates of interest were rising, and for more than a generation they remained high. This meant that if dwellings were to be let at rents which the workers could afford to pay they had to be smaller and less durable than those of the eighties. The rows of ill-built, back-to-back houses, into which the rapidly growing population of the towns was pressed, were largely the product of wartime conditions.

After 1815 matters were made worse by the influx of Irish, who, gregarious by instinct, crowded into the seaports and the towns of the North. Careful estimates made by members of the Manchester Statistical Society in the middle thirties led to the conclusion that about one-sixth of the families in Manchester were Irish, and that the percentage of the people living in cellars was 11·75. In Liverpool, where again there were many Irish, no less than 15 per cent of the inhabitants were in cellars. But in the newer towns, which were the special creation of the industrial revolution, conditions were far less grim. In Bury, where there were few Irish (and few hand-loom weavers), only 3·75 per cent, and in Ashton-under-Lyne only 1·25 per cent, of the people were housed in this way. In these places, the investigators reported, the houses of the workers were not only less crowded, but also better furnished and cleaner than those of the cities.

An historian has written of 'the disasters of the industrial revolution'. If by this he means that the years 1760–1830 were darkened by wars and made cheerless by dearth, no objection can be made to the phrase. But if he means that the technical and economic changes were themselves the source of calamity the opinion is surely perverse. The central problem of the age was how to feed and clothe and employ generations of children outnumbering by far those of any earlier time. Ireland was faced by the same problem. Failing to solve it, she lost in the forties about a fifth of her people by emigration or starvation and disease. If England had remained a nation of cultivators and craftsmen, she could hardly have escaped the same fate, and, at best, the weight of a growing population must have pressed down the spring of her spirit. She was delivered, not by her rulers, but by those who, seeking no doubt their own narrow ends, had the wit and resource to devise new instruments of production and new methods of administering industry. There are today on the plains of India and China men and women, plague-ridden and hungry, living lives little better, to outward appearance, than those of the cattle that toil with them by day and share their places of sleep at night. Such Asiatic standards, and such unmechanized horrors, are the lot of those who increase their numbers without passing through an industrial revolution.

Bibliography (revised, 1996)

The aim of this bibliography is to provide the modern reader with a guide both to older literature of enduring value and to more-recent scholarship, especially to recent texts and to work which contains extensive historiographical and bibliographical commentary. It can thus be used as a springboard for further reading. It should be regarded as a supplement to, rather than a substitute for, the original and revised bibliographies which accompanied earlier editions of the book. Particular emphasis is placed upon works which add to our understanding of those aspects of economic and social change which preoccupied Ashton. Important books and articles which involve debates and issues new since Ashton's day are also highlighted.

Several major works stressing different aspects of British industrialization were published in the first half of this century and remain important. These include P. Mantoux, *The Industrial Revolution in the Eighteenth Century* (revised edn. 1961); J. H. Clapham, *An Economic History of Modern Britain*, vol. 1 (1926); and regional and sectoral studies, principally: A. P. Wadsworth and Julia de L. Mann, *The Cotton Trade and Industrial Lancashire, 1600–1780* (1920); H. Heaton, *The Yorkshire Woollen and Worsted Industries* (1921); W. H. B. Court, *The Rise of the Midland Industries, 1600–1838* (1938); A. H. John, *The Industrial Development of South Wales, 1750–1850* (1950); H. Hamilton, *The Industrial Revolution in Scotland* (1932); J. D. Chambers, *The Vale of Trent, 1670–1800*, Supplement, *Economic History Review* (1957); T. S. Ashton, *Iron and Steel in the Industrial Revolution* (1924); T. S. Ashton and J. Sykes, *The Coal Industry of the Eighteenth Century* (1929); E. M. Sigsworth, *Black Dyke Mills*. The classic text on women also pre-dates Ashton: I. Pinchbeck, *Women Workers and the Industrial Revolution* (1930).

  More-recent research has successively estimated and revised indices of national income, industrial output, capital formation, productivity growth, and other macro-economic indicators for the eighteenth and nineteenth centuries, principally: Phyllis Deane and W. A. Cole, *British Economic Growth, 1688–1959* (1962); C. Feinstein and S. Pollard (eds.), *Studies in Capital Formation in the United Kingdom* (1988); C. Feinstein, 'Capital Formation in Great Britain', in P. Mathias and M. M. Postan (eds.), *Cambridge Economic History of Europe* (1978); N. F. R. Crafts, *British Economic Growth* (1985). Debates about the reliability and revision of these estimates and the interpretation to be placed upon them can be found in articles in learned journals. Amongst the most interesting are: J. Mokyr, 'Has the Industrial Revolution been Crowded Out?', J. G. Williamson, 'Debating the Industrial Revolution', and N. F. R. Crafts, 'British Economic Growth, 1700–1850: Some Difficulties of Interpretation', all in *Explorations in Economic History*, 24 (1987); N. F. R. Crafts, 'British Industrialisation in an International Context', *Journal of Interdisciplinary History*, 19 (1989); R. V. Jackson, 'Rates of Industrial Growth During the Industrial Revolution', *Economic History Review*, 45 (1992); J. Hoppit, 'Counting the Industrial Revolution', *Economic History Review*, 43 (1990); M. Berg and P. Hudson, 'Rehabilitating the Industrial Revolution', *Economic History Review*, 45 (1992).

Recent text-books which cover British industrialization from a broader perspective and have useful historiographical commentaries include: Maxine Berg, *The Age of Manufactures* (2nd edn., 1994); J. Rule, *The Vital Century: England's Developing Economy, 1714–1815* (1992) and *Albion's People* (1992); Pat Hudson, *The Industrial Revolution* (1992); M. J. Daunton, *Progress and Poverty: An Economic and Social History of Britain, 1700–1850* (1995). Important essay collections covering a spread of themes and containing surveys and interpretations by experts include: R. Floud and D. N. McCloskey (eds.), *The Economic History of Britain since 1700*, vol. 1 (2nd edn., 1994); J. Mokyr (ed.), *The British Industrial Revolution: An Economic Perspective* (1993); P. K. O'Brien and R. Quinault (eds.), *The Industrial Revolution and British Society* (1993); J. Langton and R. J. Morris (eds.), *Atlas of Industrialising Britain, 1780–1914* (1986); P. Mathias and J. A. Davis (eds.), *The First Industrial Revolutions* (1989); Pat Hudson (ed.), *Regions and Industries: A Perspective on the Industrial Revolution in Britain* (1989); and D. C. Coleman, *Myth, History and the Industrial Revolution* (1992), which reproduces classic essays by Coleman written over the last forty years.

Demographic history has become a major industry since Ashton's day, and the literature is particularly extensive on the relationship between population growth and industrialization in Britain (and elsewhere). The landmark study on England is E. A. Wrigley and R. S. Schofield, *The Population History of England and Wales, 1541–1871* (1981), many of the arguments of which are neatly summarized in E. A. Wrigley, 'The Growth of Population in Eighteenth Century England: A Conundrum Resolved', *Past & Present*, 98 (1993). For a different approach to the roots and implications of changes in nuptiality and fertility, see D. Levine, *Reproducing Families: The Political Economy of English Population History* (1988). For renewed emphasis on the role of mortality change see: R. Woods, 'The Effects of Population Redistribution on the Level of Mortality in 19th Century England and Wales', *Journal of Economic History*, 45 (1985); A. Mercer, *Disease, Mortality and Population in Transition: Epidemiological–Demographic Change in England since the Eighteenth Century as Part of a Global Phenomenon* (1990); R. Floud, K. Wachter, and A. Gregory, *Height, Health and History: Nutritional Status in the United Kingdom, 1750–1980* (1990). On the relationship between population growth, migration, urbanization, and economic change, see essays in E. A. Wrigley, *People, Cities and Wealth* (1987); A. Redford, *Labour Migration in England, 1800–1820* (1926); P. Clark and D. Souden, *Migration and Society in Early Modern England* (1987); P. Corfield, *The Impact of English Towns, 1700–1800* (1982); J. G. Williamson, *Coping with City Growth During the British Industrial Revolution* (1990); R. Woods, *The Population of Britain in the Nineteenth Century* (1992).

Much of the study of earlier forms of industry in recent years has been influenced by theorizing about proto-industrialization. For a short survey of this literature, see L. A. Clarkson, *Proto-industrialisation: The First Phase of Industrialisation?* (1985). Also M. Berg, P. Hudson, and M. Sonenscher (eds.), *Manufacture in Town and Country Before the Factory* (1983); D. Levine, *Family Formation in an Age of Nascent Capitalism* (1977); P. Hudson, *The Genesis of Industrial Capital: A Study of the West Riding Wool Textile Industry* c.*1750–1850* (1986); P. Hudson, 'Proto-industrialization in England', in S. C. Ogilvie and M. Cerman (eds.), *European Proto-industrialization* (1996), as well as Mantoux (1928) and Berg (1994) as above. For regionally based studies of industrializing areas, see K. Wrightson and D. Levine, *The Making of Industrial Society: Whickam, 1560–1765* (1991) and D. Rollison, *The Local Origins of Modern Society: Gloucestershire, 1500–1800* (1992). Much research has also been done upon the interface between agriculture and industry since Ashton's day. That this issue would figure centrally in any modern analysis is thanks principally to the work of A. H. John and E. L. Jones, some of whose research is reproduced in E. L. Jones (ed.), *Agriculture and Economic Growth in England* (1967); also, more recently, to K. D. M. Snell, *Annals of the Labouring Poor: Social Change and Agrarian England, 1660–1900* (1985); M. Overton, *The Agricultural Revolution* (1996); E. A. Wrigley, *Continuity, Chance and Change: The Character of the Industrial Revolution in England* (1988) and *People, Cities and Wealth* (1987); R. C. Allen, *Enclosure and the Yeoman* (1992); P. K. O'Brien, 'Agriculture and the Home Market for English Industry, 1660–1820', *English Historical Review*, 344 (1985). For detailed and authoritative overall surveys, see G. E. Mingay (ed.), *Agrarian History of England and Wales*, vol. 6 (1989). For a lively debate raging in the 1970s and 1980s about the importance of agrarian class structure for economic development, see T. H. Aston and C. H. E. Philbin, *The Brenner Debate* (1985). A survey and bibliography of the ongoing debate about the impact of enclosure is provided by M. Turner, *Enclosures in Britain, 1750–1830* (1984), whilst more recent key work and bibliographical references are to be found in Snell (1986), Overton (1996), and J. M. Neeson, *Commoners: Common Right, Enclosure and Social Change in England, 1700–1820* (1993).

On aspects of capital formation, capital supply, banking, and credit see: L. S. Presnell, *Country Banking During the Industrial Revolution* (1956); Hudson (1986); J. Hoppit, *Risk and Failure in English Business, 1700–1800* (1987); M. Collins, *Banks and Industrial Finance in Britain, 1800–1939* (1991). On the role of state revenue raising and expenditure, see J. Brewer, *The Sinews of Power* (1989) and P. K. O'Brien, 'The Political Economy of British Taxation, 1660–1815', *Economic History Review* 41 (1988), and *Power with Profit: The State and the Economy, 1688–1815* (1991). On the impact of the Napoleonic Wars, see H. T. Dickinson (ed.), *Britain and the French Revolution* (1989); P. K. O'Brien, 'The Impact of the Revolutionary and Napoleonic Wars, 1793–1815, on the Long-Run Growth of the British Economy', *Fernand Braudel Centre Review*, 12 (1989).

Very different but excellent analyses of technological change can be found in D. S. Landes, *The Unbound Prometheus* (1969); C. Macleod, *Inventing the Industrial Revolution* (1988); G. N. Von Tunzelmann, *Steam Power and British Industrialisation to 1860* (1978) and, in wider perspective, J. Mokyr, *The Lever of Riches: Technological Creativity and Economic Progress* (1990). Earlier classic work by J. Schumpeter and S. Kuznets is also worth consulting in following up Ashton's arguments. On innovation in the organizing and disciplining of labour, see S. Pollard, *The Genesis of Modern Management* (1965) and Berg, *Age of Manufactures*. And on the creation of new regional and sectoral concentrations of industry and corresponding development of regional identities, see Langton and Morris, *Atlas*; P. Hudson, *Regions and Industries*; J. Langton, 'The Industrial Revolution and the Regional Geography of England', *Transactions of the Institute of British Geographers*, 9 (1984).

By far the biggest growth-area of research and writing on British industrialization since Ashton's day has been the impact of economic development upon the living standards, way of life, culture, and politics of the lower orders. The pivotal work to which all others refer and which influenced a generation and more of interpretations was E. P. Thompson's *The Making of the English Working Class* (1963), followed more recently by *Customs in Common* (1991), which contains some older classic articles as well as newer work. Other key contributions on specific aspects of change include: essays in F. M. L. Thompson (ed.), *The Cambridge Social History of Britain*, vols. 1–3 (1990); D. Hay, P. Linebough, J. Rule, E. P. Thompson, and C. Winslow (eds.), *Albion's Fatal Tree: Crime and Society in Eighteenth Century England* (1975); J. M. Neeson (1993); L. D. Shwarz, *London in the Age of Industrialisation: Entrepreneurs, Labour Force, Living Conditions* (1992); A. J. Randall, *Before the Luddites: Custom, Community and Machinery in the English Woollen Industry* (1991); J. Foster, *Class Struggle in the Industrial Revolution* (1974); T. Koditschek, *Class Formation and Urban Industrial Society: Bradford, 1750–1850* (1990); J. Bohstedt, *Riots and Community Politics in England and Wales, 1790–1810* (1983). An account of the impact of industrialization upon many aspects of economic and social life can be found in J. Rule, *The Labouring Classes in Early Industrial England* (1986). On trade-unionism, see J. Rule (ed.), *British Trade Unionism, 1750–1850* (1988), whilst L. A. Clarkson (ed.), *British Trade Union and Labour History: A Compendium* (1990) has sections by A. E. Musson on 'British Trade Union, 1800–1850' and by Elizabeth Roberts on 'Women's Work, 1840–1940', as well as an introduction by Clarkson and a useful full bibliography. On the standard-of-living debate since Ashton, see articles in A. J. Taylor (ed.), *The Standard of Living in Britain in the Industrial Revolution* (1975); more recently, P. Lindert and J. G. Williamson, 'English Workers' Living Standards During the Industrial Revolution: A New Look', *Economic History Review*, 36 (1983); J. G. Williamson, *Did British Capitalism Breed Inequality?* (1985); S. Horrell and J. Humphries, 'Old Questions, New Data and Alternative Perspectives:

Families' Living Standards in the Industrial Revolution', *Journal of Economic History*, 52 (1992). For debates about consumption and its role in industrialization, see H. Perkin, *The Origins of Modern English Society* (1969); J. Brewer, N. McKendrick, and J. H. Plumb, *The Birth of Consumer Society: The Commercialisation of Eighteenth Century England* (1982); L. Weatherill, *Consumer Behaviour and Material Culture in Britain, 1660–1760* (1988); J. Brewer and R. Porter (eds.), *Consumption and the World and Goods* (1993).

The following references analyse change in women's lives during industrialization and have full bibliographies: J. Rendall, *Women in an Industrialising Society, 1750–1880* (1990); Berg (1995); Hudson, 'Women and Industrialisation' and other essays in J. Purvis (ed.), *Women's History in Britain, 1850–1945: An Introduction* (1995); C. Hall, *White, Male and Middle Class* (1994); P. Sharpe, 'Continuity and Change: Women's History and Economic History in Britain', *Economic History Review*, 48 (1995); D. Valenze, *The First Industrial Woman* (1995); S. Horrell and J. Humphries, 'Women's Labour Force Participation and the Transition to the Male Breadwinner Family, 1790–1865', *Economic History Review*, 48 (1985) contains recent research results, whilst B. Taylor's classic work, *Eve and the New Jerusalem* (1983), and A. Clark's *The Struggle for the Breeches: Gender and the Making of the British Working Class* (1995) consider the position of women in relation to debates about class and the development of industrial and social protest.

Good starting-points for the study of entrepreneurship and the lives and culture of the industrial and commercial bourgeoisie are: P. Payne, *British Entrepreneurship in the Nineteenth Century* and H. Perkin (1969). More-recent works include L. Davidoff and C. Hall, *Family Fortunes: Men and Women of the English Middle Class* (1987); R. J. Morris, *Class, Sect and Party: The Making of the British Middle Class: Leeds, 1820–50* (1990); J. Smail, *The Origins of Middle Class Culture: Halifax, Yorkshire, 1660–1780* (1994); A. J. Kidd and R. W. Roberts, *City, Class and Culture: Studies of Social Policy and Cultural Production in Victorian Manchester* (1985); J. Wolff and J. Seed (eds.) *The Culture of Capital: Art, Power and the 19th Century Middle Class* (1988). For references on *Laisser-faire*, the state, and administration, see A. J. Taylor, *Laissez-faire and State Intervention in Nineteenth Century Britain* (1972), which summarizes the available research to that date and has a good bibliography. For later contributions in this area, see H. Perkin, 'Individualism and Collectivism in Nineteenth Century Britain: A False Antithesis', *Journal of British Studies*, 17 (1977) and Eric J. Evans, *The Forging of the Modern State: Early Industrial Britain, 1783–1870* (1983).

For the role of the state in the eighteenth century see J. Brewer, *The Sinews of Power* (1989), and P. K. O'Brien, 'The political economy of British taxation 1660–1815' *Economic History Review*, 41 (1988).

On merchanting and foreign trade, see S. D. Chapman, *Merchant Enterprise in Britain From the Industrial Revolution to World War I* (1992); J. M. Price, 'What Did Merchants Do? Reflections on British Overseas Trade, 1660–1790' *Journal of Economic History*, 49 (1989); R. G. Wilson, *Gentleman Merchants: The Merchants Community in Leeds, 1700–1830* (1971); D. Farnie, *The Cotton Industry and the World Market, 1815–1896* (1979); R. Davis, *The Industrial Revolution and British Overseas*

Trade (1979); P. J. Cain and A. G. Hopkins, *British Imperialism: Innovation and Expansion, 1688–1914* (1993). On economic fluctuations, Ashton's own volume remains a classic: *Economic Fluctuations in England* (1959); also A. D. Gayer, W. W. Rostow, and A. J. Schwartz, *The Growth and Fluctuations of the British Economy, 1790–1850: An Historical, Statistical and Theoretical Study of Britain's Economic Development* (1953); D. Aldcroft and P. Fearon (eds.), *British Economic Fluctuations, 1790–1939* (1972); and not least, J. Hoppit, *Risk and Failure in English Business: 1700–1800* (1987).

Index

OXFORD

MORE OXFORD PAPERBACKS

This book is just one of nearly 1000 Oxford Paperbacks currently in print. If you would like details of other Oxford Paperbacks, including titles in the World's Classics, Oxford Reference, Oxford Books, OPUS, Past Masters, Oxford Authors, and Oxford Shakespeare series, please write to:

UK and Europe: Oxford Paperbacks Publicity Manager, Arts and Reference Publicity Department, Oxford University Press, Walton Street, Oxford OX2 6DP.

Customers in UK and Europe will find Oxford Paperbacks available in all good bookshops. But in case of difficulty please send orders to the Cash-with-Order Department, Oxford University Press Distribution Services, Saxon Way West, Corby, Northants NN18 9ES. Tel: 01536 741519; Fax: 01536 746337. Please send a cheque for the total cost of the books, plus £1.75 postage and packing for orders under £20; £2.75 for orders over £20. Customers outside the UK should add 10% of the cost of the books for postage and packing.

USA: Oxford Paperbacks Marketing Manager, Oxford University Press, Inc., 200 Madison Avenue, New York, N.Y. 10016.

Canada: Trade Department, Oxford University Press, 70 Wynford Drive, Don Mills, Ontario M3C 1J9.

Australia: Trade Marketing Manager, Oxford University Press, G.P.O. Box 2784Y, Melbourne 3001, Victoria.

South Africa: Oxford University Press, P.O. Box 1141, Cape Town 8000.

HISTORY IN OXFORD PAPERBACKS
TUDOR ENGLAND
John Guy

Tudor England is a compelling account of political and religious developments from the advent of the Tudors in the 1460s to the death of Elizabeth I in 1603.

Following Henry VII's capture of the Crown at Bosworth in 1485, Tudor England witnessed far-reaching changes in government and the Reformation of the Church under Henry VIII, Edward VI, Mary, and Elizabeth; that story is enriched here with character studies of the monarchs and politicians that bring to life their personalities as well as their policies.

Authoritative, clearly argued, and crisply written, this comprehensive book will be indispensable to anyone interested in the Tudor Age.

'lucid, scholarly, remarkably accomplished . . . an excellent overview' *Sunday Times*

'the first comprehensive history of Tudor England for more than thirty years' Patrick Collinson, *Ob-/server*

OPUS

General Editors: Walter Bodmer,
Christopher Butler, Robert Evans,
John Skorupski

CLASSICAL THOUGHT

Terence Irwin

Spanning over a thousand years from Homer to Saint Augustine, *Classical Thought* encompasses a vast range of material, in succinct style, while remaining clear and lucid even to those with no philosophical or Classical background.

The major philosophers and philosophical schools are examined—the Presocratics, Socrates, Plato, Aristotle, Stoicism, Epicureanism, Neoplatonism; but other important thinkers, such as Greek tragedians, historians, medical writers, and early Christian writers, are also discussed. The emphasis is naturally on questions of philosophical interest (although the literary and historical background to Classical philosophy is not ignored), and again the scope is broad—ethics, the theory of knowledge, philosophy of mind, philosophical theology. All this is presented in a fully integrated, highly readable text which covers many of the most important areas of ancient thought and in which stress is laid on the variety and continuity of philosophical thinking after Aristotle.

Oxford
Paperback
Reference

THE CONCISE OXFORD DICTIONARY
OF POLITICS

Edited by Iain McLean

Written by an expert team of political scientists from Warwick University, this is the most authoritative and up-to-date dictionary of politics available.

* Over 1,500 entries provide truly international coverage of major political institutions, thinkers and concepts

* From Western to Chinese and Muslim political thought

* Covers new and thriving branches of the subject, including international political economy, voting theory, and feminism

* Appendix of political leaders

* Clear, no-nonsense definitions of terms such as veto and subsidiarity